The STORY OF America in CARTOONS

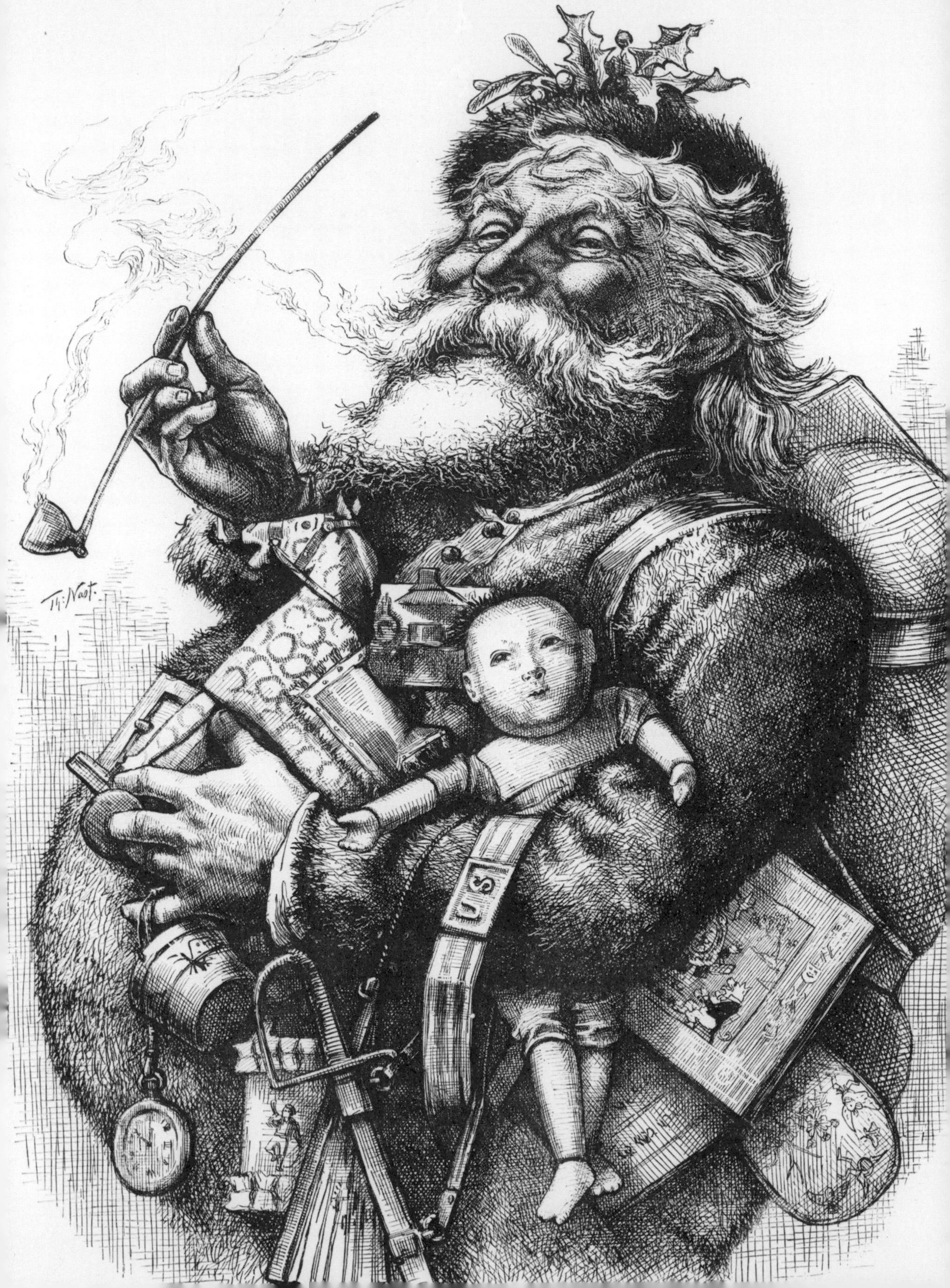
Th: Nast.
U S

The STORY OF America in CARTOONS

Edited by Tony Husbabd

ARCTURUS

Princeton University woman baseball player (1905, Library of Congress) by Louise Clarke

This edition published in 2015 by Arcturus Publishing Limited
26/27 Bickels Yard, 151–153 Bermondsey Street,
London SE1 3HA

ISBN: 978-1-78404-825-9
AD004424US

Printed in China

CONTENTS

MUST LIBERTY'S LIGHT GO OUT?
ESPIONAGE BILL
LIBERTY

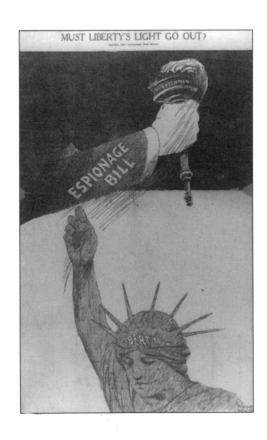

INTRODUCTION

The US is an amazing, complex country, positively youthful compared to the venerable nations of Asia and Europe, but boy has it had an impact over its short life!

Energetic, vibrant, bullish and bristling with self-belief, this is a nation that has changed, and continues to change, the world. Its people are warm, generous and extrovert – they've come from every continent to make this vast melting pot of a country their home, and to make America what it is today.

That's what this book chronicles: the birth, growing pains and coming of age of the world's most powerful nation seen through the eyes of cartoonists. From Day One, American politics have been like an endless bar-room brawl as the cartoons here illustrate, a neverending battle of ideas – it's called Democracy.

When you come to think about it, there's no better shortcut to understanding history than a book of cartoons. They add up to a concise visual diary of events, sharply observed, clear and uncluttered, funny rather than cloying, with no room for maudlin sentiment, jingoism or bombast – in fact, those are exactly the qualities they seek to undermine. There's no need for 1,000-

ABOVE: A warning about the consequences of the Stamp Act in 1765, which required American colonists to pay tax on printed documents, including playing cards, to help pay for British troops in America. This was considered to be taxation without representation.

RIGHT: Brother Jonathan, precursor of Uncle Sam, straddles the entrance to the Philadelphia World Fair, 1876. He symbolized a 'nation of equal and autonomous states', while Uncle Sam represented Washington.

page tomes. In a few lines and a few words, a cartoon defines the moment perfectly.

In this book you will see how life was and is: how a colony freed itself from the stifling embrace of 18th-century Europe and forged its own identity, a place which cartoonists first characterized through the identity of yokel businessman Brother Jonathan, a figure which morphed into

statesman Uncle Sam as the nation came together around Washington. The idea of independence marked the beginning of the American Dream and soon the politicians, philosophers and campaigners began writing a Constitution to match the yearning of the people for freedom.

From the very first settlers driving the Native Americans in front of them in their

Copyright 1876, by Currier & Ives, N.Y.

R. & IVES

125 NASSAU ST. NE

THE STRIDE OF A CENTURY.

covered wagons to successive waves of immigrants, American history has never lacked for incident. This book begins with the War of Independence – where one cartoon shows an American viper encircling the army base of the pompous English (the viper predated the stars 'n' stripes as an early symbol of America) – and takes in the Civil War, the Gold Rush, World Wars I and II, as well as the Cold War and the struggle for Civil Rights along the way. America has always been divided – North v South, black v white, rich v poor – and the American cartoonist has always had his hands full making sense of the rights and wrongs, and grievances, of each community versus every other.

Luckily the country has had outstanding talent to light the way forward, artists such as Thomas Nast, Joseph Keppler, W. A. Rogers, Clifford Berryman, Homer Davenport, Bill Mauldin, D. R. Fitzpatrick and Herb Block to name but a few. Sad to report, we will never

This cartoon from 1861-1862 is thought to be the first political cartoon showing an elephant confronting a donkey, animals later adopted as the symbols of the Republicans and Democrats. The dandified donkey (standing for the Confederacy and Jefferson Davis) suddenly appreciates the military might of the Union as the gallows awaits behind him. During the Civil War, 'Seeing the elephant' came to mean experiencing combat.

JEFF. SEES THE ELEPHANT.

Two skeletons perform a dance of death on the body of a victim of
one of the many steam boiler explosions which occurred on railway
locomotives and marine transport or in power plants. Here, blame is
heaped upon officials who failed to enforce the safety rules. (1883)

know the names of many of the artists who drew the first cartoons in this history.

True to its origins as an underdog, America likes to do things on its own terms and has built its own way of life from the collective cultures that have landed on its shores. Perhaps that's why the rest of the world has slavishly adopted so much from the US: its love of the car and big business, Hollywood, consumerism, travel, celebrity, and all the technologies it leads in.

American heroes are often the world's heroes too: Martin Luther King, JFK and Joe Louis are all larger than life characters. And where would things be without US love of music and dance? America was the birthplace of jazz and the blues; it gave us the Charleston too – see also the cartoon on

BELOW: By 1890 when this cartoon appeared in *Judge* magazine, many Native Americans had lost their hunting grounds. This image portrays a corrupt federal agent who has been lining his pockets with money intended as restitution.

THE REASON OF THE INDIAN OUTBREAK.
General Miles declares that the Indians are starved into rebellion.

ABOVE: Ex-rancher Teddy Roosevelt leads a fantasy posse of Paul Revere, Tam O'Shanter, Don Quixote, Icabod Crane and the Pony Express, among others, by Louis M. Glackens (1909).

Toward a New World!

ABOVE: Herb Block ingeniously finds a connection between the years 1492 and 1942 as America rides to the rescue of the Old World, which was then under massive threat from the Nazis, the Japanese and their Axis allies.

page 138, 'The Dancing Marathon' ('the first hundred hours are the worst!').

Finally I'd like to consider two cartoons by the brilliant Engelhardt: one shows a pistol with a number of bullets labeled 'homicide', 'accidents', 'hold-ups' and so on, with the caption 'American Roulette' (p.187). This was drawn in 1971 and sadly the gun debate still rages. In the other from 2001 (p.190), the specter of death hovers over the Twin Towers.

These images point to a new reality for America; the old certainties are gone. This is an interesting and dangerous time not only for America but for the world. Rest assured, however, American cartoonists will keep rising to their task as watchdogs, keeping the Land of the Free on the straight and narrow.   **Tony Husband**

PEACE — PEACE — PEACE

AMERICA

ATLANTIC

1

2

3

4
Accept Peace on any Terms.

5
Here must 20.000. Saving in a Year.

6
I will live in a Famous quite you &c.

7
I coming a bundle of poor banished our Expences will save

I coming in a high pin of each kingdom

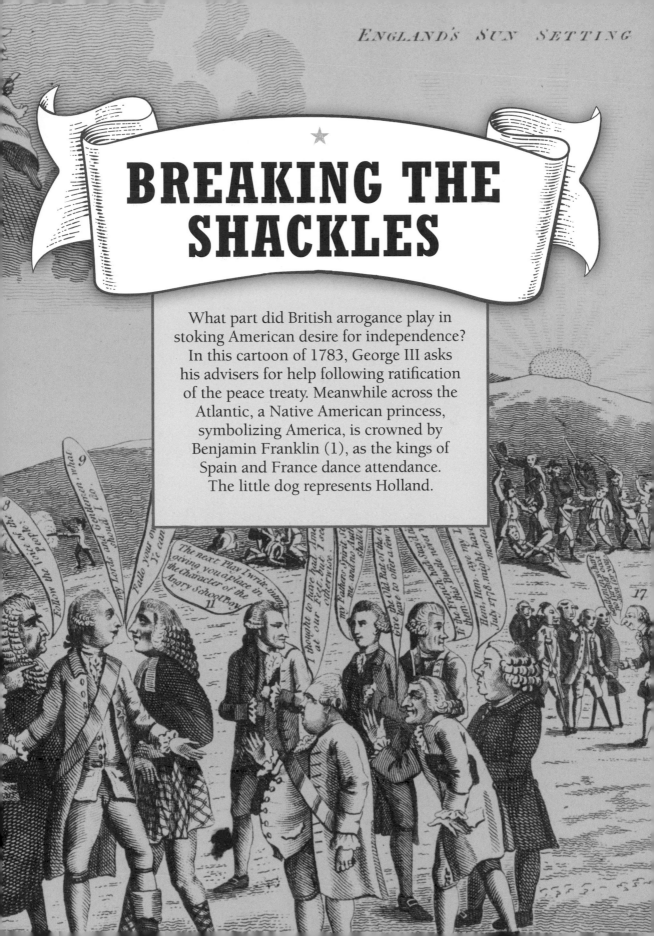

BREAKING THE SHACKLES

What part did British arrogance play in stoking American desire for independence? In this cartoon of 1783, George III asks his advisers for help following ratification of the peace treaty. Meanwhile across the Atlantic, a Native American princess, symbolizing America, is crowned by Benjamin Franklin (1), as the kings of Spain and France dance attendance. The little dog represents Holland.

Their triumph about him

C. Smith bound to a tree to be shott to death
1607

Captain John Smith played a part in establishing Jamestown, the first permanent British settlement in the Americas and perhaps the beginning of the British Empire. He was also responsible for launching the dubious myth of the 'good Indian who saved the white man', claiming Pocahontas, the chief's daughter, saved his life when he was captured and her father decided to execute him. It became the talk of London.

The map of Virginia in 1670 as drawn up by Augustine Herman, Bohemian merchant and cartographer. Herman divided his time between Maryland and New Amsterdam, later called New York. There's an interesting inset image of the Powatan people with a reference to John Smith who was their prisoner. The Powatan, also known as the Virginia Algonquians, were native to Virginia.

The Salem Witch Trials began in 1692 after young girls in Salem, Massachusetts claimed to be possessed by the devil and accused local women of witchcraft. Mass hysteria erupted and died down quickly enough, but not before 150 men, women and children had been accused. Many were hanged. It was Puritan belief that evil existed as an entity in itself, but this episode led Americans to be wary of including religion in the Constitution.

Probably designed by Benjamin Franklin, this image of a chopped-up snake, calling on American colonists from South Carolina to New England to unite against the French and Native Americans, is thought to be the first editorial cartoon to appear in an American newspaper, the *Pennsylvania Gazette* (on 9 May 1754). The rattlesnake came to be a symbol of America's struggle for freedom.

'Common-Wealth – the Colossus' (1766): In this English cartoon, poor William Pitt, the 'great commoner', needs stilts to cope with all his responsibilities between Britain and the New World; it's making his position rather precarious. In a 15-line poem, he is mocked for building a castle in the air, accepting a peerage and for the Repeal of the Stamp Act. And following America's example, the Irish seem to be getting uppity too! One of Pitt's stilts, in New York, is labeled 'Sedition'; the other, in London, 'Popularity'.

In the fall of 1774, the British extended their blockade of Boston to include New York, which led to New Yorkers withdrawing all co-operation from the occupying forces. British soldiers started disguising themselves as civilians to visit town. Here, New York barber Jacob Vredenburgh, a Son of Liberty, stops shaving British Navy captain John Crozer halfway through the job when a messenger arives with an official communique, giving away the customer's identity. Interesting details in this engraving include the names of Sons of Liberty on wig boxes and portraits of English defenders of civil liberties on the wall, a pointed reminder to those across the Atlantic.

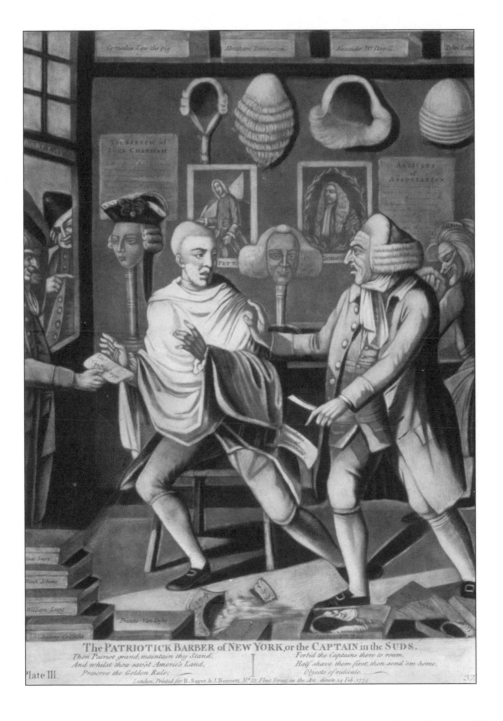

THE BOSTONIANS PAYING THE EXCISEMAN, OR TARRING AND FEATHERING.

Left: Five men pour tea into the mouth of John Malcolm, Boston Commissioner of Customs and a hardline British loyalist, after tarring and feathering him under the Liberty Tree in January 1774. This was a humiliation that stopped just short of serious injury. This print shows the Boston Tea Party going on behind them, an event that actually took place four weeks earlier in December 1773.

Left: 'Bunkers Hill or America's head dress', 1776, by Matthew Darly: Cartoon published in London after the Battle of Bunker Hill which satirizes High Roll hairstyles then fashionable among wealthy women and the impertinence of Americans in thinking they could defy British troops with their makeshift forces and frivolous tactics. In a narrow victory for the British, more than a thousand men were killed or wounded.

THE TAKEING OF MISS MUD ILAND.

LEFT: A crude English woodcut with a caricature of Molly Pitcher, the composite heroine figure of American Independence, firing a cannon from between her legs at British warships attacking Fort Mifflin on Mud Island. The fortress overlooking the confluence of the Schuylkill and Delaware rivers surrendered after a seven-week siege in 1777.

BELOW: Lord Mansfield (with whip) and George III are in an open chaise being pulled towards a chasm which represents war with the American colonies by two horses labeled 'Pride' and 'Obstinacy'. These animals are trampling all over the 'Magna Charta' and the Constitution as America burns in the distance. This cartoon, which contains many topical allusions to the corruption of those surrounding the monarch, appeared in the *Westminster Magazine* in 1775.

The Political Cartoon, for the Year 1775.

Poor old England endeavoring to reclaim his wicked American Children. Gat therefore is England meaning & force to go with a Staff.

Above: Published in London just over a year after the Continental Congress voted for independence and a month before General Burgoyne surrendered at Saratoga, this American cartoon from 1777 shows Poor Old England with his peg leg struggling to control his unruly colonial children, one of whom is firing a pea-shooter at him.

Right: George III is thrown by a horse he can't control despite the scourge he holds with its ferocious lashing attachments. Behind is a minuteman bearing a flag symbolizing the 13 colonies. The meaning of this cartoon which was published and printed in London is interesting. Is it designed to encourage the Americans or to incite the British into action? Popular opinion in Britain over the American war was divided. In the cities, support for the rebels was as strong as for the government.

THE HORSE AMERICA, throwing his Master.

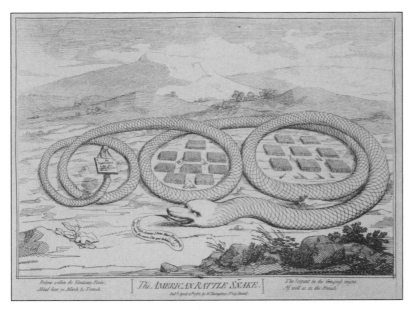

LEFT: The rattlesnake was the symbol used on American flags before the stars 'n' stripes and here it lies with its coils wrapped around British troops at Yorktown and Saratoga as legendary cartoonist James Gillray seeks to warn his compatriots in England about the futility (in 1782) of continuing to suppress the American colonies. They could never be defeated.

BELOW: A Spaniard and a Frenchman lead George III (on a leash) and Lord Shelburne towards a building marked 'Inquisition' for preliminary talks on a peace treaty through a gateway of spears, from which topple the British lion, a crown and a unicorn, signifying the change in ownership. Behind them is an American patriot with a 13-lash whip, one for each colony, and a comedy Dutchman in tow. (1783)

RIGHT: Encouraged by Spain, France and Holland, a cross-dressing 'Mrs General George Washington' gives Britannia 13 lashes, one for each colony. He says: 'Parents should not behave like Tyrants to their children.' She replies: 'Is it thus my Children treat me?' Truly, few things are more upsetting than a break-up in the family, and the British had become terribly accustomed to seeing America as their wayward offspring. (1783)

Mrs General Washington. Bestowing thirteen Stripes on Britania.

RIGHT: A European view of the American Revolution from 1783 and a parody of an earlier British print by John Dixon ('The Oracle', 1774). Here Old Father Time uses a magic lantern to show representatives of Asia, Africa, America and Europe a vision of a tea pot exploding above a bed of burning tea-tax stamps fanned by a French cockerel and propeling a deadly rattlesnake towards terrified British troops as American soldiers advance behind. Quite complicated really!

The TEA-TAX-TEMPEST, or OLD TIME with his MAGICK-LANTHERN.

James Gillray's savage attack on Tom Paine, author of the radical *Rights of Man* and a founding father of the USA, who is pictured as a ragged, Frenchified tailor measuring up a giant crown for a 'new pair of Revolution Breeches'. Inspired by the French Revolution of 1789, Paine wanted to shake up political systems worldwide. (1791)

He in a trice struck Lyon thrice
Upon his head, enrag'd sir.

Who seiz'd the tongs to ease his wrongs,
And Griswold thus engag'd sir.

Congress Hall,
in Philada. Feby. 15. 1798.

LEFT: 'Zion Besieg'd and attack'd' (1787):' This crazy, chaotic print shows a large citadel (on the right) being beseiged by legions of politicians, demons, bankers and beasts. 'Zion' represents the 1776 Constitution of Philadelphia, which was remarkably democratic and restricted the governor's power. No wonder the politicians didn't like it. Relentless campaigns against it resulted in a more conservative constitution in 1790.

BELOW LEFT: The fight that burst out in 1798 on the floor of Congress, then in Philadelphia, between Matthew Lyon of Vermont and Roger Griswold of Connecticut. A few weeks before, Lyon had spat tobacco juice into Griswold's eye after an exchange of insults. Griswold, who started the brawl, is armed with a hickory walking stick, while Lyon wields a pair of fire tongs.

BELOW: In July 1790 Congress decided to move the seat of federal government from New York to a new city to be built in the District of Columbia (Washington), with Philadelphia serving as interim capital until 1800. This cartoon is a cynical satire on the opportunities for profit to be made from a traveling capital, with a devil positioned by a fork in the river leading to Philadelphia.

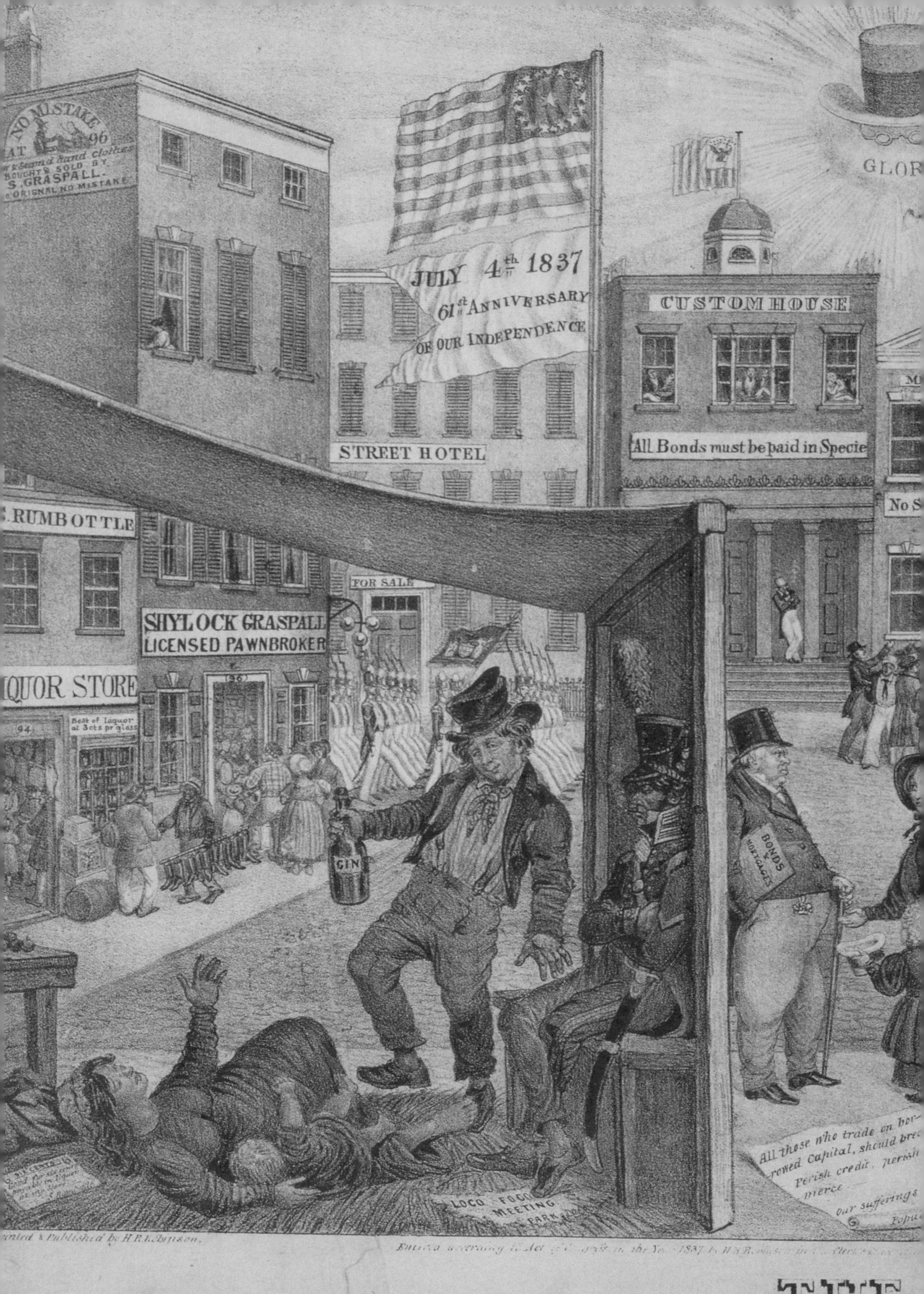
NO MISTAKE
AT 96
S. GRASPALL.
JULY 4th 1837
61st ANNIVERSARY
OF OUR INDEPENDENCE
CUSTOM HOUSE
STREET HOTEL
All Bonds must be paid in Specie
RUMBOTTLE
FOR SALE
SHYLOCK GRASPALL
LICENSED PAWNBROKER
IQUOR STORE
94
Best of Liquor at 3cts pr glass
96
GIN
BONDS & MORTGAGES
No S
LOCO FOCO MEETING PARK
All those who trade on borrowed Capital, should brea
Perish credit, perish
merce
GLOR
Printed & Published by H.R. Robinson.

THE

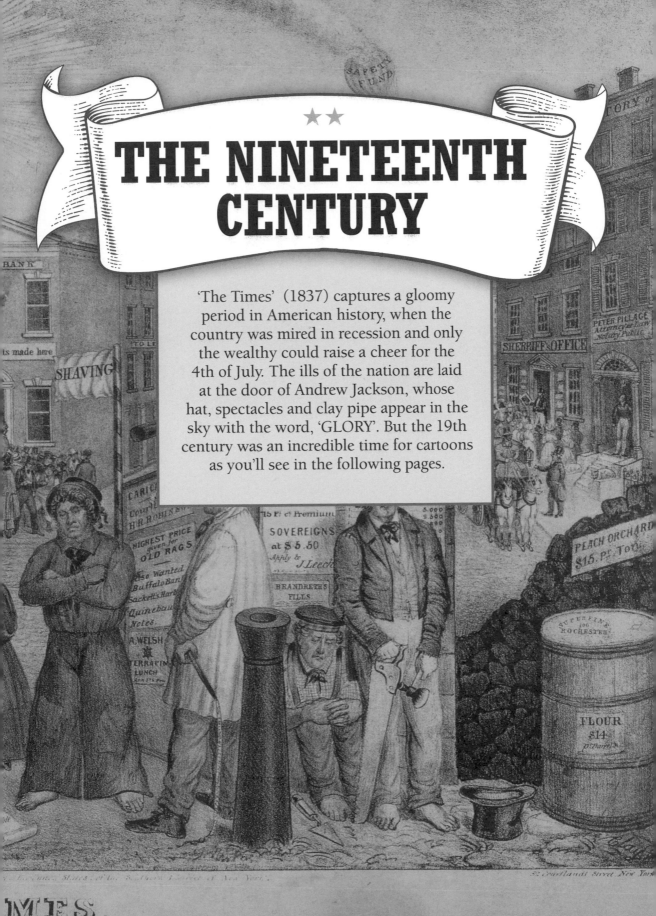

THE NINETEENTH CENTURY

'The Times' (1837) captures a gloomy period in American history, when the country was mired in recession and only the wealthy could raise a cheer for the 4th of July. The ills of the nation are laid at the door of Andrew Jackson, whose hat, spectacles and clay pipe appear in the sky with the word, 'GLORY'. But the 19th century was an incredible time for cartoons as you'll see in the following pages.

RIGHT: A rather sinister image by David Claypole Johnston (1834), showing Henry Clay of Kentucky sewing up President Andrew Jackson's mouth. The pair were engaged in a long-running feud over the future of the Second Bank of the United States and Clay kept trying to censure Jackson. Below the cartoon is a slight misquote from Shakespeare's *Hamlet*: 'Clay might stop a hole, to keep the wind away.'

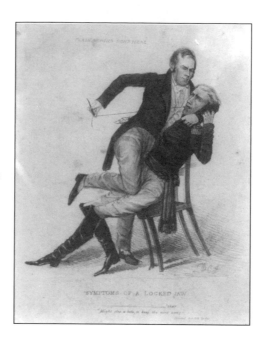

A NEW MAP
Exhibiting

ABOVE: George III is given a black eye and a bloody nose by 4th President James Madison as reference is made to British shipping losses in the War of 1812 and to the recent capture of the brig *Boxer* by the US ship *Enterprise* in September 1813. George refers to Madison as Brother Jonathan, who in turn seems to be mistaking the English monarch for John Bull. (by W. Charles, c.1813)

The map below symbolizes the 1828 election race between Andrew Jackson (alligator) and John Quincy Adams (turtle). Watched by the Winebago people on the skyline, it shows a weird tug-of-war between the two men, which Jackson won by a landslide. He created the modern Democratic party, thus inaugurating the Second Party system.

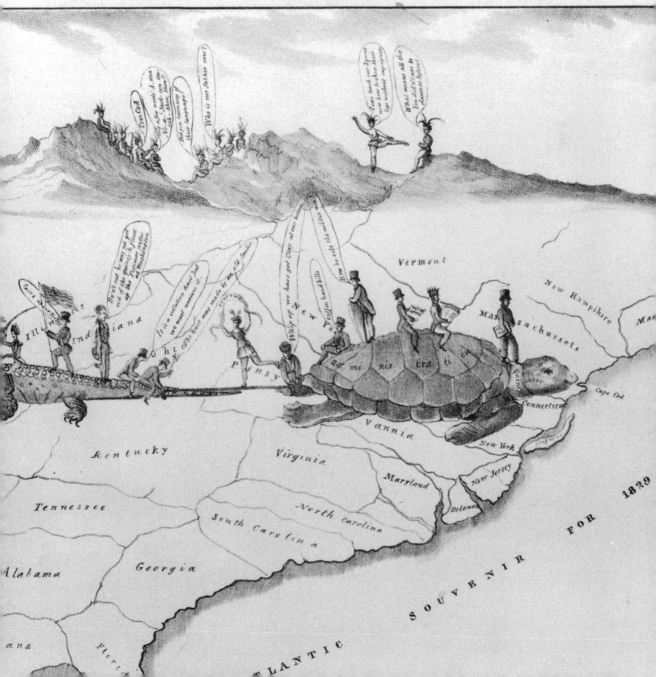

Right: The Loco Focos were radical Democrats who, opposed by the Whigs, demanded equal rights for practically everybody. Here, the conflict is characterized through warring street vendors. A boy selling Loco-Foco brand matches is punched in the nose by a Whig newspaper seller as a passing black chimney-sweep taunts the Loco Focos, 'Does Fanny know you're out?', a scathing reference to Frances Wright ('Fanny'), the radical reformer of the time. In essence, this cartoon is calling the Democrats wimps, suggesting that the Whigs are tougher and more masculine – not to mention the fact that the Loco Focos don't even have the support of marginalized figures such as the black sweep. (By H. R. Robinson, 1836)

Below: The big fight between Nicholas Biddle and 'man of the people' Andrew Jackson over the future of the Second Bank of the United States. Jackson wanted to revoke its charter because, he said, it 'made the rich richer and the potent more powerful'. Biddle is supported by Mother Bank with her bottle of port; in the other corner is 'Joe Tammany' with his whiskey. In 1841, the bank was liquidated after a severe bout of financial turbulence.

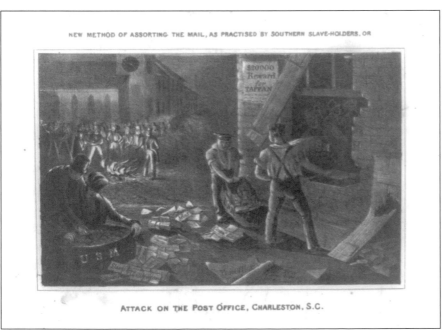

A raid on the Charleston post office carried out by a pro-slavery mob in 1835. They were on the lookout for abolitionist letters and newspapers which they were more than happy to intercept and destroy.

"WHAT? YOU YOUNG YANKEE-NOODLE, STRIKE
YOUR OWN FATHER!"

An English cartoon by John Leech (1846) shows a tiny James K. Polk, US
president, squaring up to big John Bull over the disputed territory of Oregon
Country – British Columbia, Oregon, Washington, Idaho and parts of Montana
and Wyoming. The Oregon Treaty of 1846 set the border at the 49th Parallel.

SLAVERY AS IT EXISTS IN AMERICA.

SLAVERY AS IT EXISTS IN ENGLAND.

Left: A lithograph from John Haven (1850) favorably comparing the condition of slaves in America with the conditions of the poor in industrial England. With the added aim of keeping British noses out of American affairs, this was another salvo in the continuing propaganda war between Northern abolitionists and Southern slavers.

Right: 'Jump Jim Crow' was a song-and-dance caricature of black people designed to flatter then current notions of white superiority. The act was first performed by white actor, Thomas Dartmouth Rice, in blackface and ragged clothes in 1828 to satirize Andrew Jackson's populist policies. By 1838, 'Jim Crow' had become a much-used pejorative term and the later racial segregation laws in some Southern states were dubbed 'Jim Crow Laws'.

JIM CROW.

THE LAND OF LIBERTY.

RECOMMENDED TO THE CONSIDERATION OF "BROTHER JONATHAN."

James K. Polk is known as the 'least well known consequential president' due to the quiet but effective way he went about his business. However, he threatened Britain with war over Oregon Country and *Punch* cartoonist Richard Doyle responded by showing him as a dissolute Brother Jonathan in 1847, pointing out paradoxes in the Land of Liberty, which included slavery and the forced annexation of Texas after the Mexican–American War. What would George Washington have made of it all?

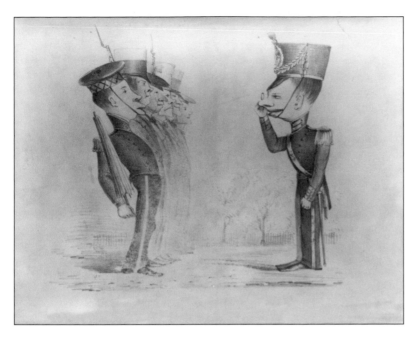

LEFT: 'Volunteers for Texas. As You Were' (1846) by Fanny Palmer and Thomas Odham: A scornful view of the quality of volunteers for the Mexican War. A large percentage of enlistees were Irish immigrants, many of whom had no military experience. They're mostly wearing civilian clothes, while the officer is a chinless wonder.

BELOW: 'Knock'd into a Cock'd Hat' (1848) by Nathanial Currier: A cannon ball marked with the face of Zachary Taylor and shot out of a cannon marked 'Philadelphia Convention' knocks Democrat nominee Lewis Cass backward into a cocked hat. This cartoon was correctly predicting that Cass had no chance against the newly nominated Whig candidate Zachary Taylor.

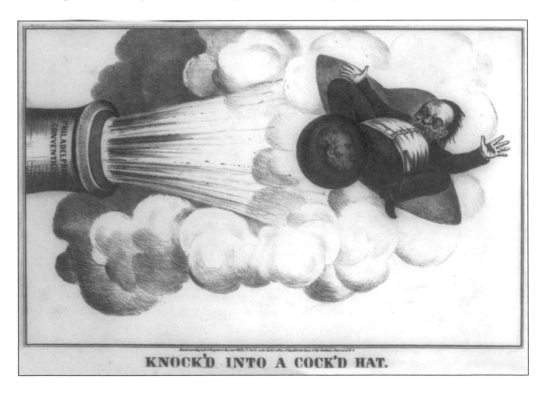

KNOCK'D INTO A COCK'D HAT.

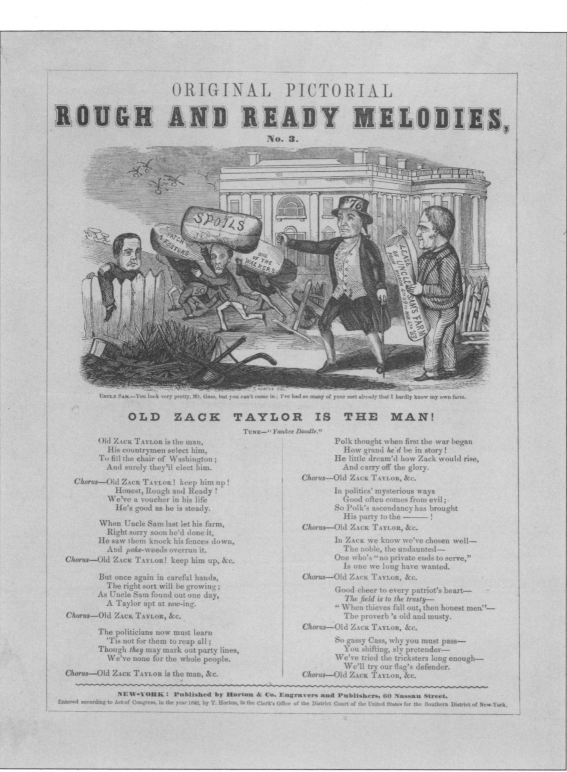

A triumphalist Whig campaign songsheet from 1848, which shows Uncle Sam throwing Democratic riff-raff out of the White House to make way for Zachary Taylor, who had just become the 12th president of the USA. Democrat Lewis Cass is attempting to sneak in over the fence.

LOLA HAS COME!

ENTHUSIASTIC RECEPTION OF LOLA BY AN AMERICAN AUDIENCE.

AN AVAILABLE CANDIDATE.
THE ONE QUALIFICATION FOR A WHIG PRESIDENT.

ABOVE: Lola Montez was the stage name of an Irish dancer and actress who had an affair with Franz Liszt and was mistress to Ludwig I of Bavaria. In 1848, she fled revolution in the German states and ended up in the US, where her repertoire included the erotic 'Spider Dance'. Here, a Puritan ogles her through his fingers, a man in the theater box observes her over his newspaper and the greedy house manager has a 'half the house' agreement in his pocket. She caused quite a stir!

LEFT: A scathing view of Zachary Taylor before he captured the Whig nomination for the presidency. Seated on a pyramid of skulls with a bloodstained sword, this is a reference to the bloody part he played as a soldier in the American–Mexican War. (by Nathaniel Currier, 1848)

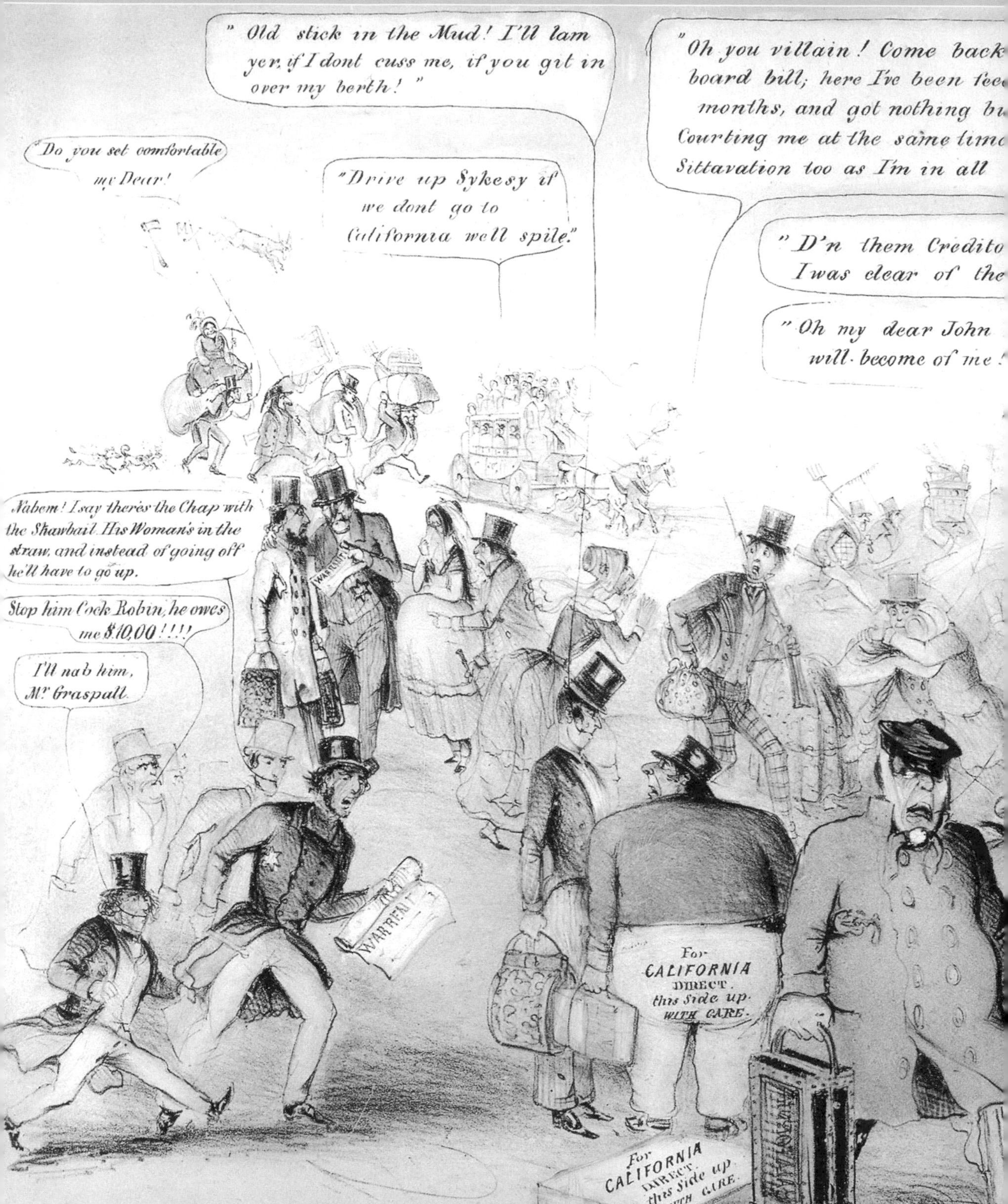
"Old stick in the Mud! I'll lam yer, if I dont cuss me, if you git in over my berth!"
"Oh you villain! Come back board bill; here I've been fee months, and got nothing bu Courting me at the same time Sittavation too as I'm in all
"Do you set comfortable my Dear!
"Drive up Sykesy if we dont go to California well spile."
"D'n them Credito I was clear of the
"Oh my dear John will become of me!
Nabem! I say theres the Chap with the Shawbail. His Woman's in the straw, and instead of going off he'll have to go up.
Stop him Cock Robin, he owes me $10,00!!!!
I'll nab him, Mr Graspall.
WARRENT
For CALIFORNIA DIRECT. this side up. WITH CARE.
For CALIFORNIA DIRECT. this side up WITH CARE.
Manning

The Gold Rush

The discovery of gold in 1848 brought 300,000 prospectors racing toward California as Gold Fever infected America. Between 1846 and 1852, the population of San Francisco grew from 200 to over 36,000. Indeed the Gold Rush proved the making of California, which became the 31st state in 1850. Roads were built as the population expanded and the railroad soon followed. In this lithograph by New Yorker H. R. Robinson, the '49-ers' are satirized as fly-by-nights and ne'er-do-wells.

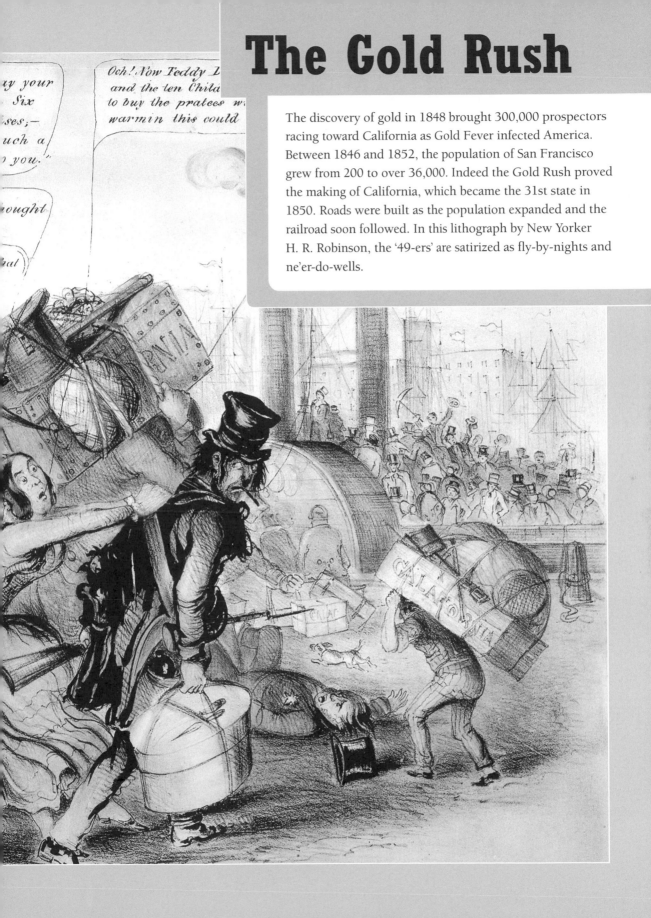

"THE USED-UP MAN"—

GRAND PATENT

FROM THE ATLANTIC TO THE PACIFIC, THROUGH IN NO TIME. *The principle of in safety their place of destination. Reverse the above and they are back again.*

This image first appeared in *Pen Knife Sketches* by Alonzo Delano (1853), a satirical account of conditions during the Gold Rush. The artist was Charles Nahl who fled from the third French Revolution in 1848 with his family, and abandoned panning for gold in the Sierra foothills for life as a portrait painter in Sacramento and then San Francisco. He made a fortune painting fancy, flattering portraits of prospectors who had struck lucky to send home to loved ones in Europe and 'back East'. The haunted figure above was the other sort of prospector, and there were many more like him!

A crazy contraption designed by H. R. Robinson to get those seeking a 'glint of color' (gold) over to California in the fastest time possible (1849). No other place on Earth seemed to offer such amazing possibilities of enrichment to those without skills, and all sorts of people came running from all sorts of places, hoping to stake their claim in the great land and mineral grab.

THE NEW YORK METROPOLITAN POLICE.
A PICTORIAL ANALYSIS OF THE REPORT TO THE LEGISLATURE.

1. These gentlemen, finding the garroting business on the decline, resolve to become guardians of law and order, and enter the Metropolitan Police.

2. Policemen are but men, and when young and fascinating women happen to get into the police-stations, who can blame them if they are civil and gallant?

3. As to poor devils, houseless wretches, with no good looks, and steeped in poverty and misery, can a high-bred policeman be expected to cringe to such as these? No, no; let them eat the bread of sorrow.

BELOW: A sudden outbreak of goodwill between John Bull and Brother Jonathan after joining hands across the ocean, so to speak, with the laying of a telegraph cable between Valentia Island, Ireland and Newfoundland by US steamer *Niagara* and British steamer *Agamemnon*. They're saying such nice things about each other too!

ABOVE: With ironic wording, the author of these images of 1859 chides the New York Metropolitan Police for its corruption and brutality. Battering anyone who got in their way with nightsticks, the capital's cops extorted millions from gambling dens, brothels and after-hours saloons in the city's filthy, vice-ridden underbelly.

THE LAYING OF THE CABLE—JOHN AND JONATHAN JOINING HANDS.

RIGHT: The Kansas–Nebraska Act (1854) created Kansas and Nebraska, opening new lands for settlement but leaving incomers to vote on whether they wanted slavery or not. This led to violent confrontations between the anti-slavery freesoilers and their opponents which presaged the Civil War. This dramatic image blames Democrats for the problem.

FORCING SLAVERY DOWN THE THROAT OF A FREESOILER

BELOW: 'A slight idea of the comfort of having plenty of stages' (1859): If you think the traffic in NYC is bad now, you should have seen it 150 years ago. You couldn't move for horse-drawn vehicles. In 1850, they brought in the Broadway Squad, forerunners of today's traffic cops.

Uncle Abe

the Union must and
Shall be Preserved

The Civil War

The American Civil War (1861–65) was fought between the breakaway 'Confederate' states in the South and the 'Union' in the North. A key issue was the proposed extension of slavery into western territories. This Confederate cartoon dates from the start of the conflict. It casts Abraham Lincoln ('Uncle Abe') as a cat struggling to catch the Southern states (the mice) as they flee the Union to join the Confederacy.

This cartoon from 1861 was originally titled 'PHUNNY PHELLOW', a reference to Jefferson Davis who is taking on Abraham Lincoln in a 'Great Fight for the Championship between the Southern Fillibuster and the Western Railsplitter'. In the orginal caption, editor Horace Greeley (of the *New York Tribune*) asks: 'Why don't you go in Abe? What's the use o' waiting for an openin' any longer?' Lincoln replies to the bald Greeley: 'Keep Cool and let your hair grow Horace! I know wot I'm about. I want to tire him out!'

LEFT: The First Battle of Bull Run (1861) was the first major conflict of the Civil War and both sides were evenly matched with 18,000 poorly trained troops. The Confederates won. This image is seen from the point of view of a 'Copperhead', a Northern Democrat supporting the Confederacy.

THE VOLUNTARY MANNER IN WHICH SOME OF THE SOUTHERN VOLUNTEERS ENLIST.

Prodded forward at bayonet point, a volunteer arrives in a Southern recruiting office, where the walls are covered in misleading propaganda posters, a small dog is urinating on a drunk, a model of 'Old Abe' is hanging from a noose and there are ridiculous bits of household bric-a-brac 'captured by the Southern Navy'. This is a piece of Northern propaganda by Thomas Worth, New York, 1862.

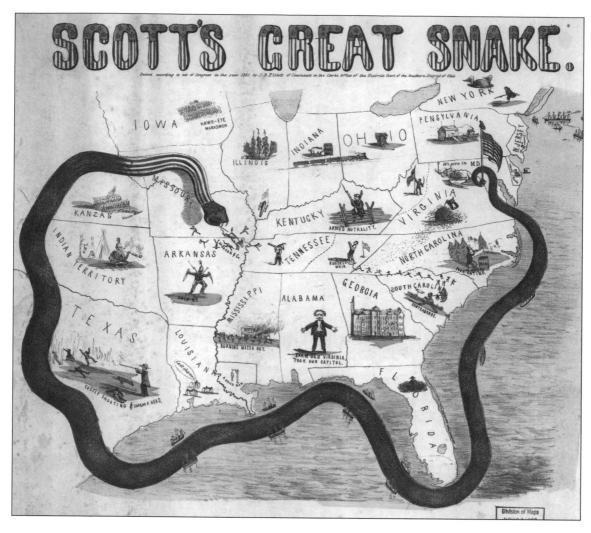

SCOTT'S GREAT SNAKE.

ABOVE: A mocking view by J. B. Elliott from Cincinnati (1861) of Winfield Scott's so-called 'Anaconda Plan' at the beginning of the Civil War to firm up Washington's defenses, blockade the bits of the Gulf Coast and Atlantic Coast controlled by the Confederacy, and to launch a combined naval and land force along the Mississippi to split the Confederacy in two.

RIGHT: In June 1861 the state legislature of Missouri voted to secede from the Union to become the 12th Confederate state, but the meeting had been called during outbreaks of violence and not all the members could arrive in time. As a result the secession was not recognized by the Unionists in the state, who formed a separate government. Missouri thus had two separate state governments, sending representatives to both the United States Congress and the Confederate Congress.

Poor deluded Miss-Souri takes a Secession bath, and finds it much hotter than she expected!

THE "RAIL SPLITTER" AT WORK REPAIRING THE UNION.

LEFT: True to his humble origins, Abraham Lincoln worked as a farmhand, soldier, postmaster, surveyor, tavern keeper and rail splitter before opting for politics. The idea of Lincoln as a 'rail splitter' became popular in his 1860 election campaign; he was seen as a man of the people. The image was revived in this cartoon of 1865 by Joseph E. Baker. With Republican running mate Andrew Johnson, Abe's mending the country and underlining his credentials as 'father' of the Union.

ABOVE: 'The First of May 1865, or General Moving Day in Richmond Virginia', published in 1865 following the surrender of the Southern states. Confederate leaders – Robert E. Lee, Stonewall Jackson and Jefferson Davis – move the bankrupt Confederacy out of the South, represented by a house that is now presided over by two African-American men.

THE MODERN ARK.—DRAWN BY SOL EYTINGE, FROM A SKETCH BY E. S. BISBEE.—[SEE PAGE 423.]

ABOVE: Wood engraving by Sol Eytinge from a sketch by E. S. Bisbee (1871) which paints an unflattering picture of immigrants as scrounging opportunists taking advantage of generous American hospitality. During the 1870s and 1880s, the majority came from Germany, Ireland and Britain and 70 percent of them arrived in New York City, then known as the 'Golden Door'.

RIGHT: In 1874 General Benjamin Butler, famous for his bombast, proposed an Inflation Bill to increase the supply of greenbacks (paper currency backed by government authority rather than gold or silver) by $44m to counter economic problems after the Panic of 1873. President Grant vetoed the bill and street vendors did a roaring trade in 'Beast Butler' chamber pots. (Thomas Nast, 1874)

Dubbed the 'Father of American cartoons', Thomas Nast loved nothing better than drawing William 'Boss' Tweed, corrupt leader of Tammany Hall, the Democratic political machine that was defrauding New York City out of millions. In the top image, bagman James H. Ingersoll introduces an overlarge Tweed (who's hiding Mayor Hall behind his hat) to Horace Greeley, editor of the *New York Tribune*; below, they're all passing the buck. Tweed later ran off to Cuba, where he was identified as a fugitive from justice using one of Nast's drawings. (1871)

"TO THINE OWN SELF BE TRUE."

"THESE FEW PRECEPTS IN THY MEMORY."

Above: During the debate over the Civil Rights Bill of 1875, seven African-American Congressmen offered personal testimony regarding the discrimination they suffered in public places. 'Every day, my life and property are exposed, are left to the mercy of others and will be so long as every hotel-keeper, railroad conductor and steamboat captain can refuse me with impunity,' Representative James Rapier of Alabama said. 'After all, this question resolves itself into this: Either I am a man, or I am not a man.' The original draft which would have outlawed racism across the board was watered down to make it more palatable to conservative elements, and in 1883 the Supreme Court struck it down. It was only in in the second half of the 20th century that a series of Civil Rights Acts enshrined equality in federal law. (Thomas Nast, 1875)

BELOW: A year after the Battle of Little Big Horn in Montana, when George Custer and five troops of US cavalry were massacred, Sitting Bull escaped government retribution by leading his people from their traditional hunting grounds in Montana into Canada where they came under British protection. In 1883 Sitting Bull returned to Standing Rock reservation in South Dakota, where he was killed in 1890 by Indian Agency police, who feared he would join the Ghost Dance religious movement, which aimed to remove all evil – including White settlers – from tribal lands through ritual dance and spiritual cleansing.

REVENGE IS SWEET.

"My dear, since the Government is losing so much Revenue on account of the 'Crusade on Whisky,' they are going to make it up on Tea."

In 1874 the Women's Christian Temperance Union held a national convention in Cleveland, Ohio. Their crusade against whiskey and all other forms of alcohol was being conducted with the intent of creating 'a sober and pure world'. Here Thomas Nast makes a simple, marital tit-for-tat joke out of the event.

OUR NEW SENATORS.

SECRETARY SEWARD—"*My dear Mr. Kamskatca, you really must dine with me. I have some of the very finest tallow candles and the lovliest train oil you ever tasted, and my whale's blubber is exquisite—and pray bring your friend Mr. Seal along with you. The President will be one of the party.*"

In 1859, Russia offered to sell Alaska to the USA because the territory was isolated and well nigh impossible to defend. The Alaskan Purchase finally took place after the Civil War in 1867 at a price of $7.2m (equivalent to $121m today). Until the Gold Strike in the Klondike in 1896, few Americans gave Alaska a second's thought, but the deal gave fresh impetus to the Canadian Confederation, which British Columbia joined in 1871 for fear of US annexation. In 1959 Alaska became a US state.

ABOVE: 'American Frankenstein' by Frank Bellew (1874): As they expanded, American railroad companies seemed to be running out of control, seizing great tracts of land for development, indulging in nefarious practises to gain advantage over rivals and operating politicians like puppets to trample on the rights of the people. No one knew how their activities could be curtailed…

RIGHT: A send-up of the Irish on St Patrick's Day by cartoonist Livingston 'HOP' Hopkins (1874) and published in the NY *Daily Graphic*: This seizes on the perceived characteristics of one of the largest immigrant groups in New York City, famous for providing the backbone of the NYCPD and fire brigade. The Irish may love America, but they never give up their allegiance to their native land.

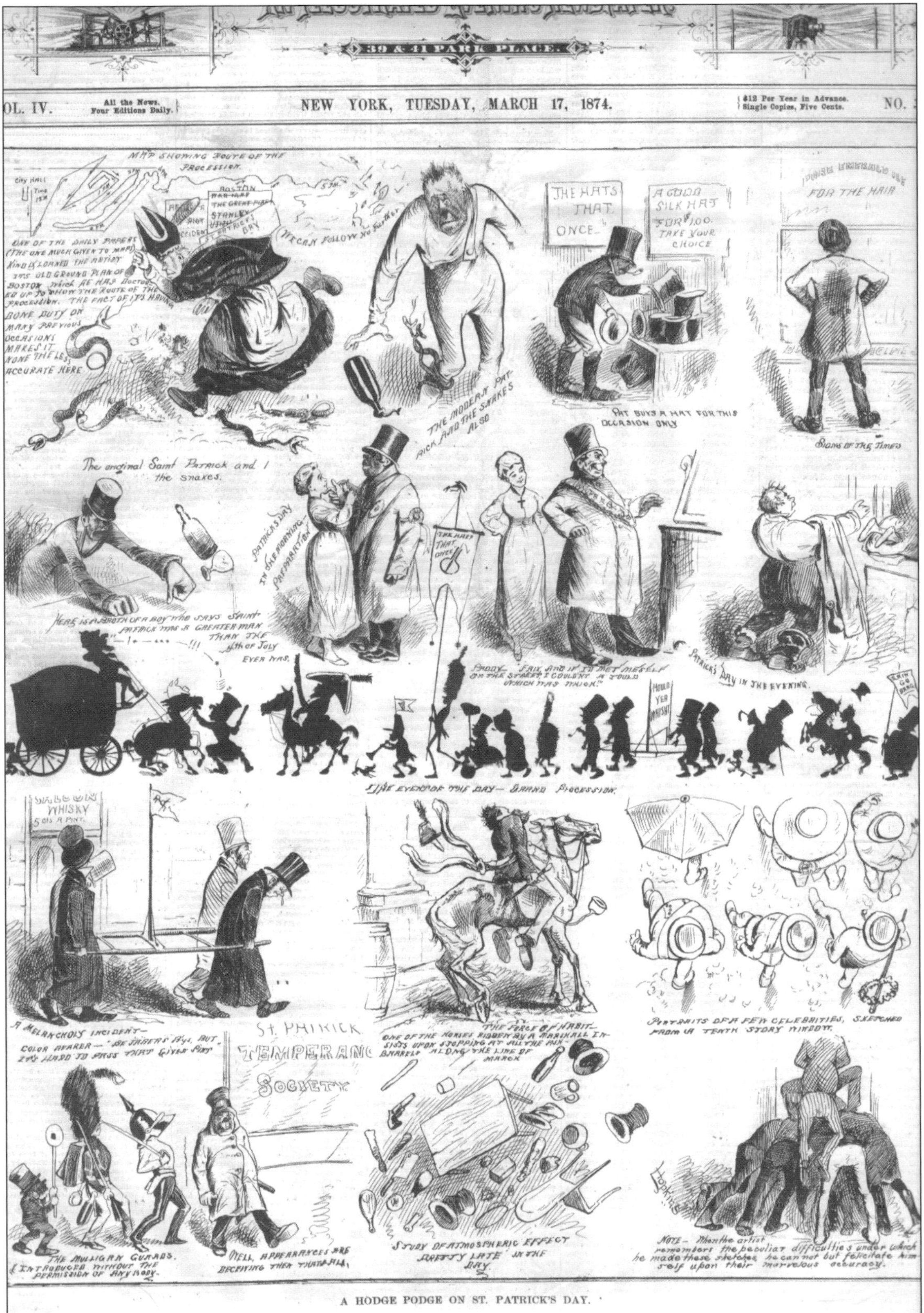
39 & 41 PARK PLACE.
OL. IV. All the News. Four Editions Daily.
NEW YORK, TUESDAY, MARCH 17, 1874.
$12 Per Year in Advance. Single Copies, Five Cents.
NO.
MAP SHOWING ROUTE OF THE PROCESSION.
City HALL
ONE OF THE DAILY PAPERS (THE ONE MUCH GIVEN TO MAPS) KINDLY LOANED THE ARTIST ITS OLD GROUND PLAN OF BOSTON WHICH HE HAS DOCTORED UP TO SHOW THE ROUTE OF THE PROCESSION. THE FACT OF ITS HAVING DONE DUTY ON MANY PREVIOUS OCCASIONS MAKES IT NONE THE LESS ACCURATE HERE
WE CAN FOLLOW NO further
THE MODERN PAT RICK AND THE SNAKES ALSO
THE HATS THAT ONCE
A GOOD SILK HAT FOR $1.00. TAKE YOUR CHOICE
PAT BUYS A HAT FOR THIS OCCASION ONLY
FOR THE HAIR
Signs of the Times
The original Saint Patrick and the snakes.
HERE IS A BROTH OF A BOY WHO SAYS SAINT PATRICK WAS A GREATER MAN THAN THE 4th OF JULY EVER WAS.
PATRICK'S DAY IN THE MORNING PREPARATION
THE HATS THAT ONCE
PADDY — "FAIX, AND IF I'D MET MESELF ON THE STREET, I COULDN'T A TOULD WHICH WAS WHICH."
PATRICK'S DAY IN THE EVENING.
HOULD YER WHISHT
ERIN GO BRAGH
THE EVENT OF THE DAY — GRAND PROCESSION.
WHISKY 5 cts A PINT.
A MELANCHOLY INCIDENT — COLOR BEARER — "BE JABERS! AYS, BUT, IT'S HARD TO PASS THAT GIVES PINT"
THE FORCE OF HABIT — ONE OF THE HORSES RIDDEN BY A MARSHALL INSISTS UPON STOPPING AT ALL THE RUM-BARRELS ALONG THE LINE OF MARCH
PORTRAITS OF A FEW CELEBRITIES, SKETCHED FROM A TENTH STORY WINDOW.
St. PATRICK TEMPERANC SOCIETY
THE MULLIGAN GUARDS. INTRODUCED WITHOUT THE PERMISSION OF ANY BODY.
WELL, APPEARANCES ARE DECEIVING THEN THAT'S ALL.
STUDY OF ATMOSPHERIC EFFECT PRETTY LATE IN THE DAY.
NOTE — When the artist remembers the peculiar difficulties under which he made these sketches, he can not but felicitate himself upon their marvelous accuracy.
A HODGE PODGE ON ST. PATRICK'S DAY.

Left: 'Meet Old Santa Claus' (1881): Thomas Nast was largely responsible for creating the version of Santa Claus which we recognize today, a jolly, roly-poly, avuncular figure with a full white beard.

Right: A beautiful drawing of the terrible, squalid conditions in a tenement occupied by Irish immigrants in 1879, by Joseph Keppler. These buildings, also known as rookeries, were cramped and overcrowded, prone to collapse and fire; most occupants had very little direct sunlight, but by far the worst place to live was the cellar.

Below: Allegorical illustration of the Transcontinental railroad link-up at Promontory Summit, Utah, by Frank Beard (1869). Native Americans and buffaloes flee in the foreground. The title implies that the increased speed of communication and savings in shipping costs would make up for all the money and effort expended. The journey from New York to San Francisco by train took six days.

FRANK LESLIE'S ILLUSTRATED NEWSPAPER.   [MAY 29, 1869.

SAN FRANCISCO   NEW YORK

"DOES NOT SUCH A MEETING MAKE AMENDS?"

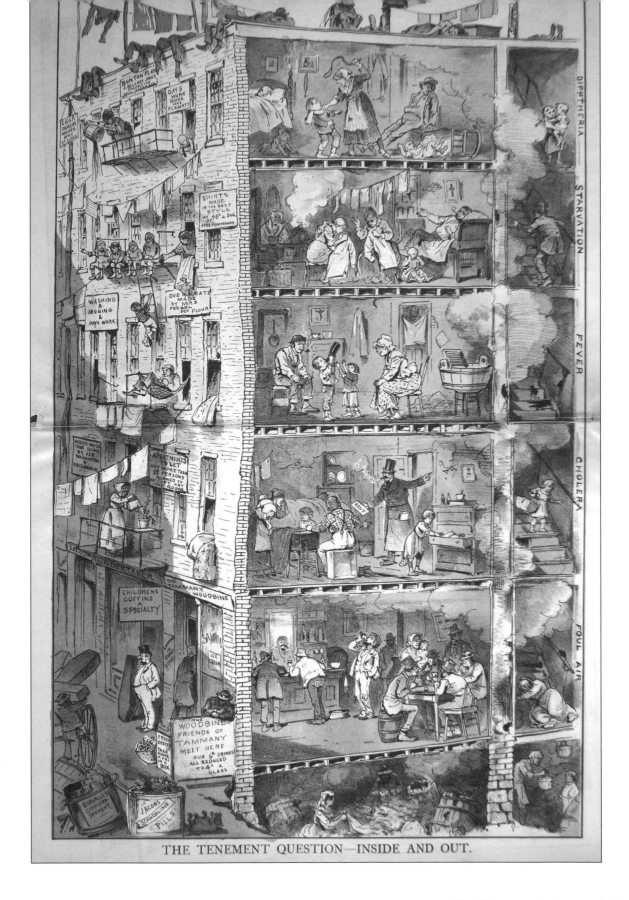

THE TENEMENT QUESTION—INSIDE AND OUT.

ABOVE: German-born Senator Carl Schurz of Missouri is portrayed as a carpetbagger by Thomas Nast (1872). Carpetbaggers were opportunistic Northerners who moved to the South during the Reconstruction period after the Civil War in order to take advantage of the political vacuum for their own gain.

THE GREAT WAR COMET OF 1861.

LEFT: Mocking image of Civil War general Winfield Scott whose features form the head of a comet which has a tail of bayonets. 'The Great Comet of 1861' was visible to the naked eye above the USA for three months of that year.

Above: 'The American Juggernaut' by Matthew Morgan (1873): The strapline reads as follows: 'Everything noble, patriotic and progressive is crushed beneath the remorseless tread of the mammoth monster of corruption, cruelty and fraud, the vampire rings of capital…' Between 1871 and 1900, an extra 170,000 miles were added to the US railroad network, which, despite this undertaking's widespread unpopularity, tied the country together, made fortunes for a select few and paved the way for settlement of the West.

'An End to Slavery' by Thomas Nast (1874): After the Civil War, Reconstruction meant there was a conscious effort to reunite the nation, but the White League and the Ku Klux Klan continued to use violence to terrorize the black population in the South. Nast had an exemplary record as a defender of the rights of minorities, except for his one big blind spot – many of his cartoons expressed contempt for the Irish community and the Catholic religion.

A GROUP OF VULTURES WAITING FOR THE STORM TO "BLOW OVER"—"LET US PREY."

ABOVE: 'A Group of Vultures Waiting for the Storm to "Blow Over" – "Let us Prey"' by Thomas Nast (1871): Sending up a speech about carpetbaggers by Horace Greeley (see image below), Nast portrays the four key Tweed Ring operators – Peter Sweeny, William 'Boss' Tweed, Richard Connolly and Oakley Hall – as vultures sitting on a ledge next to the bleached bones of New York. The Tweed Ring were big cogs in the corrupt Democratic machine that ran the city. In 1871 their many crimes were exposed by the *New York Times*. Nast had campaigned against them for years, but now he had wind in his sails. That's why Tweed tried unsuccessfully to bribe him to take a long, luxurious trip to Europe, saying: 'I don't care a straw for your newspaper articles; my constituents don't know how to read, but they can't help seeing them damned pictures!' (See also page 51.)

RIGHT: Horace Greeley, editor of the *New York Tribune*, ran for president in 1872 with the support of the Democrats in Tammany Hall, here symbolized by a jailbird with 'KKK' on his belt. Thomas Nast is pointing out the unsavoriness of the highly convenient but forced alliance between former bitter enemies, Greeley and the Democrats.

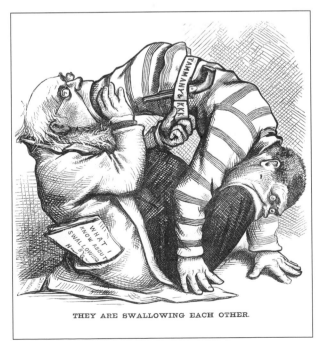

THEY ARE SWALLOWING EACH OTHER.

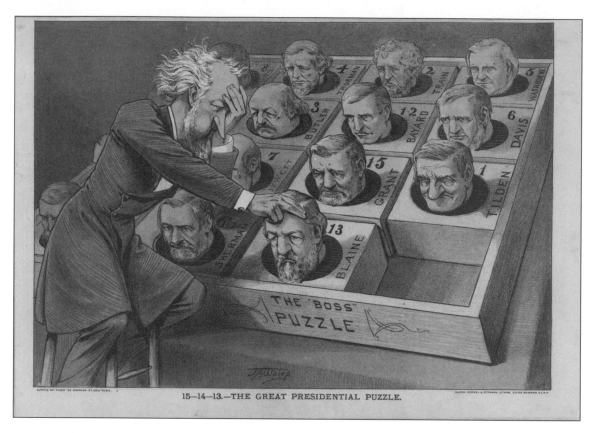

15—14—13.—THE GREAT PRESIDENTIAL PUZZLE.

THEN AND NOW.—1862 AND 1882.

ORDER Nº 11.
BY U.S. GRANT.
1862.
EXCLUDING
JEWS —
FROM THE
ARMY.—

MEETING
CHICKERING
HALL
SYMPATHY
FOR THE
PERSECUTED
JEWS
IN RUSSIA
U.S. GRANT.

ARMY ORDER Nº 11—1862

JEWISH VOTE!
1884

"OH, NOW YOU WEEP, AND I PERCEIVE YOU FEEL
THE DINT OF PITY. THESE ARE GRACIOUS DROPS."

ABOVE: Senator Roscoe Conkling of the Stalwart Group of Republicans attempts to solve a puzzle: who will be candidate for the 1880 election? In real life, after the 35th ballot, Blaine and Sherman shifted their support to 'dark horse' candidate James Garfield who defeated Winfield Scott in a close-run election. (by James Albert Wales, 1880)

RIGHT: Mark Twain discovered that if you wanted to register your book for copyright in Canada, then bizarrely you had to do so in the office of the Minister of Agriculture, which led Thomas Nast to produce the portrait opposite. Author of *Tom Sawyer*, Twain is often seen as the 'Father of the American novel'.

LEFT: Bernhard Gillam takes Ulysses S. Grant to task in 1882 for hypocrisy after he'd excluded Jews from the military district he ran in 1862, allegedly for running a black market in cotton. Now he is pursuing the Jewish vote by calling for the end of persecution in Russia.

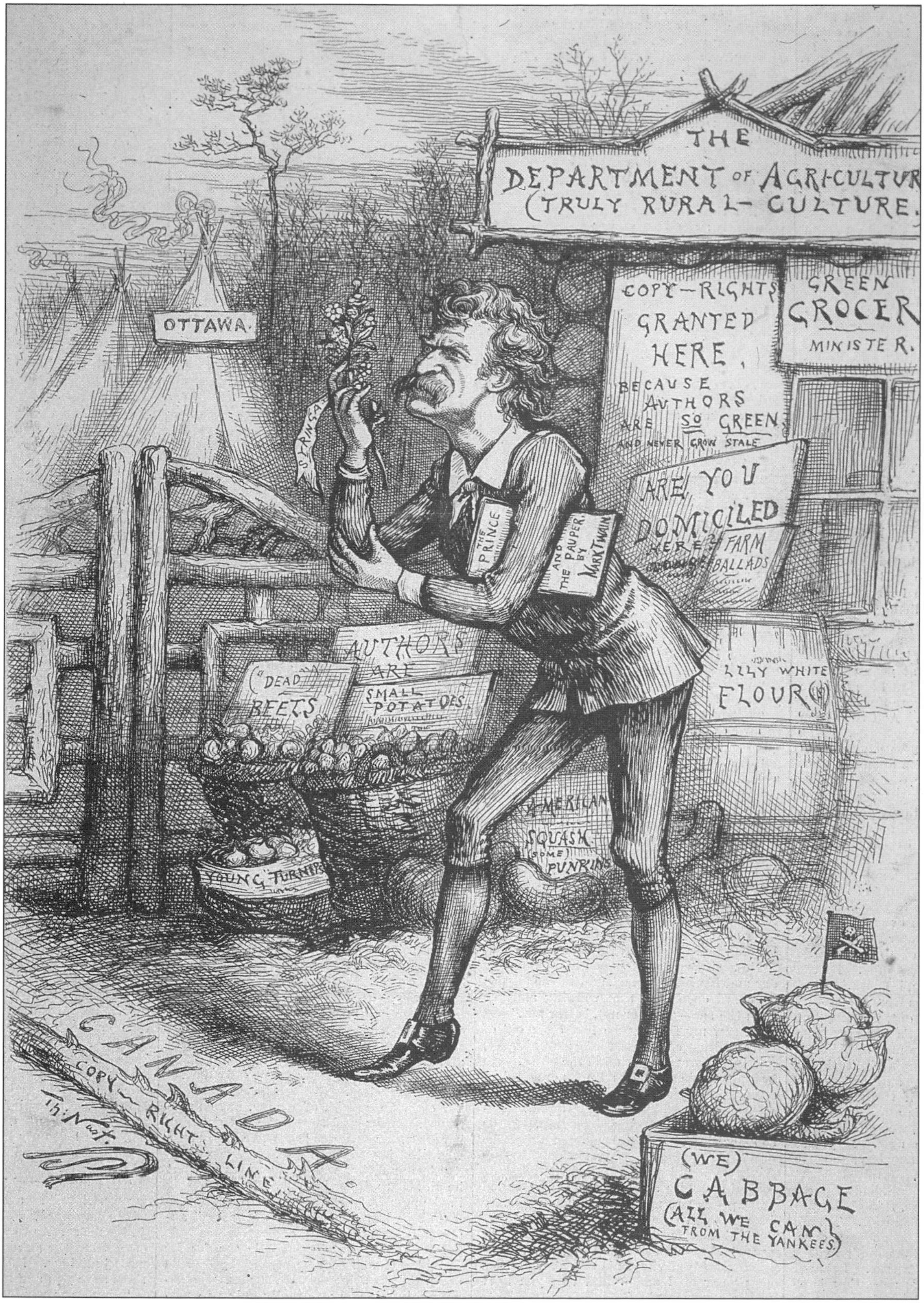
THE
DEPARTMENT OF AGRI-CULTUR
(TRULY RURAL-CULTURE.
OTTAWA
COPY-RIGHTS GRANTED HERE, BECAUSE AUTHORS ARE SO GREEN AND NEVER GROW STALE
GREEN GROCER MINISTER.
ARE YOU DOMICILED HERE?
FARM BALLADS
THE PRINCE AND THE PAUPER. BY MARK TWAIN
AUTHORS ARE SMALL POTATOES.
"DEAD" BEETS
LILY WHITE FLOUR
AMERICAN SQUASH (SOME) PUNKINS
YOUNG TURNIPS
CANADA
COPY-RIGHT LINE
(WE) CABBAGE (ALL WE CAN) FROM THE YANKEES
Th: Nast.

PUCK.

THE HOSTILES ON THE TRAIL.

"President Arthur, on his trip to the Yellowstone region, will join one of Gen. Sheridan's 'Military Exploring Parties.' There is a tradition among the Indians that you can always identify the trail of 'Little Phil's' exploring parties by the empty whiskey bottles, etc., scattered along the line of march."—*Brooklyn Eagle.*

ABOVE: President Arthur visited Yellowstone National Park in 1883 on a jolly with General Sheridan who had advocated the extermination of buffalo to make 'Plains Indians' change their nomadic existence. Native Americans are shown in an unflattering light here, but the Indian Wars were over and the authorities were slowly becoming more conciliatory.

RIGHT: Poet Oscar Wilde kicked off his 11-month tour of America in 1882 by telling customs he had 'nothing to declare but my genius' and ramped it up from there on in. In satin knee britches and silk stockings, he traveled 15,000 miles to give 140 lectures promoting aesthetics in a land heavily devoted to industrial expansion. He caused a stir wherever he went and earned himself a fortune.

OSCAR WILDE ON OUR CAST-IRON STOVES.
Another American Institution sat down on.

ABOVE: 'Monopoly Millionaires Divide Up the Country' (1882): This was a time of technological change, social upheaval and a widening gap between rich and poor. Frederick Opper shows railroad entrepreneurs sharing out the USA as European royalty watches from across the Atlantic, awaiting their offer from the fat cats.

LEFT: 'Uncle Sam Presents his Return Quota of "Assisted" Immigrants' by W. A. Rogers (c.1887): John Bull and the British Lion await a consignment of immigrants back from the USA, which includes Native Americans. This cartoon appeared in *Harper's Weekly*.

The Edison of the Past.

"Now, gentlemen, I will show you the Great Invention T[...]
Money, and here's your Share; now you see them, and now y[...]

'The Decadence of the Wizard of Menlo Park' by Joseph Keppler (1880): Inventor Thomas Edison is shown at the center of the image as a sham wizard in a makeshift cap performing the age-old shuffling cups trick. His fall from grace is charted, from brilliant scientist to a man who is using past glories to hook up with unscrupulous traders on Wall Street in a bid to finance some of his crazier inventions.

THE CHINESE PUZZLED.

"Is it because we don't do deeds like that, that *we* 'must go' and they stay?"

LEFT: 'The Chinese Puzzled' by Thomas Nast (1886): Nast lampoons the Knights of Labor, a mainly Catholic organization which supported the Chinese Exclusion Act and whose rallies often ended in violence. He's suggesting it's crazy that troublemakers and anarchists were more welcome in America than peaceful Chinese immigrants.

BELOW: By this time, travelers expected more and more convenience, so magnificent hotels were erected next to railroad stations. According to the 'American Plan', meals were included in the cost of rooms which meant demand for tables was unprecedented. (by Thomas Worth, 1884)

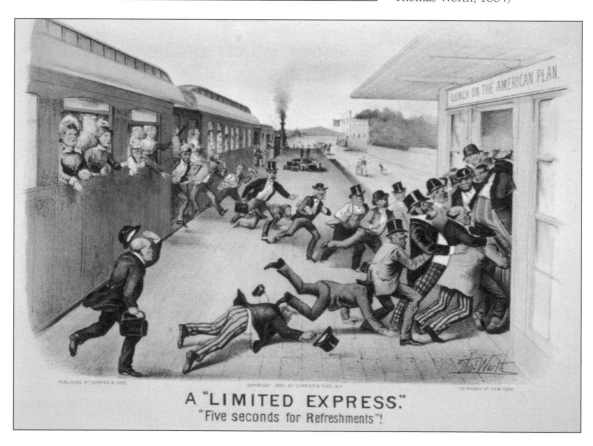

A "LIMITED EXPRESS."
"Five seconds for Refreshments"!

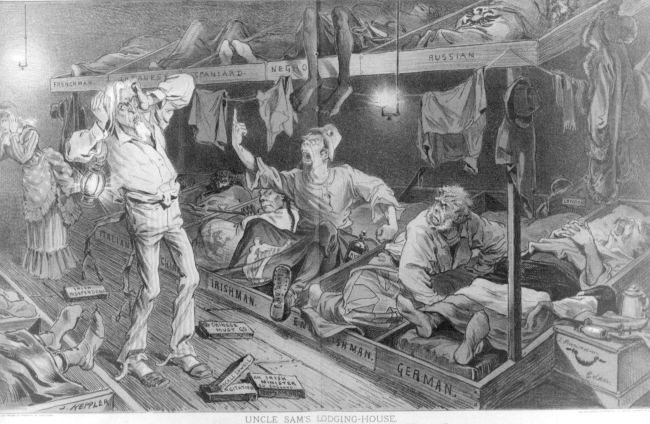

UNCLE SAM'S LODGING-HOUSE.

Uncle Sam:—"Look here, you, everybody else is quiet and peaceable, and you're all the time a-kicking up a row!"

ABOVE: 'Uncle Sam's Lodging House' by Joseph Keppler (1882): Uncle Sam is asking the Irishman to keep the noise down – 'Look here, you, everybody else is quiet and peacable and you're all the time a-kicking up a row.' The Irish made up a vociferous minority in New York City.

LEFT: A baseball match between the Democrats and the Republicans, which is a surrogate for the 1884 presidential election. James G. Blaine is pitching to Chester A. Arthur with Roscoe Conkling as umpire. Benjamin 'Beast' Butler has a handgun in his belt and the game is taking place in the 'Potomac Flats' near the White House.

The Nineteenth Century | 71

PHINEAS T. BARNUM,

BIGGEST SHOWMAN IN THE WORLD; BAR—NONE.

ABOVE: A portrait of Phineas Barnum by Edward Linley Sambourne in *Punch* (1884): Barnum is shown as a wily fox brilliant at exploiting human credulity to make money for his circus, 'The Greatest Show on Earth'. Phrenology, the belief that the formation of the skull revealed mental capacity, was very popular at the time.

RIGHT: Workers put the finishing touches to the Brooklyn Bridge in 1883. Six days after opening, a rumor that the bridge was collapsing caused a stampede, with a dozen people crushed to death. In 1884, genius of publicity Phineas T. Barnum led a procession of 21 elephants, headed by the famous 'Jumbo', across the structure to quash any remaining doubts about its stability.

FRANK LESLIE'S
ILLUSTRATED
NEWSPAPER

Entered according to Act of Congress, in the year 1883, by Mrs. FRANK LESLIE, in the Office of the Librarian of Congress at Washington.—Entered at the Post Office, New York, N.Y., as Second-class Matter.

No. 1,440.—VOL. LVI]   NEW YORK—FOR THE WEEK ENDING APRIL 28, 1883.   [PRICE, 10 CENTS. $4.00 YEARLY.
13 WEEKS, $1.07

NEW YORK.—COMPLETING A GREAT WORK—LASHING THE STAYS OF THE BROOKLYN BRIDGE.
FROM A SKETCH BY A STAFF ARTIST.—SEE PAGE 155.

FATHER KNICKERBOCKER'S TERRIB

"The combined weight of the huge buildings pressing on the lower end of Manhattan Island is estimated by experts at not less than one hundred billion p
is subjected to! If it could get free, if it should burst its confines at the edge of either river and start from under the buildings nearest the water, how terrible m
29, 1896.

LIGHT.

What a tremendous squeeze the underlying gravel, clay and sand
...aster!' From an article in the NEW YORK HERALD, November

PUCK.

THE BICYCLE PROBLEM.

ABOVE: 1895 was a highpoint of the Great Bicycle Craze. This was 'a general intoxicating, an eruption of exuberance like a seismic tremor that shook the economic and social foundations of society'. In particular, the 'New Woman' of the era was able to flaunt her independence on a bicycle along with functional attire.

LEFT: Father Knickerbocker, symbol of New York City, clings for dear life to Manhattan Island which has been upended by the sheer weight of skyscrapers built upon it. Fortunately for New Yorkers, city engineers have mostly done the sums right and this scenario from the *New York Herald*, 1896, has never come to pass.

LEFT: 'Reasonable' by Samuel D. Ehrhart (1896): Ehrhart satirized the social mores of his time in loving detail.

BELOW: Thomas Nast weighs in against 'richest man in the world' Andrew Carnegie and his attempts to break the union at his steel mill at Homestead, near Pittsburgh, in 1892. After management had locked out 3,800 workers who refused a 20 percent wage cut, they seized the mill. On 6 July, Carnegie hired in 300 Pinkerton detectives but they were repeled. Three workers and seven Pinkertons were killed. The Pennsylvania governor sent in 8,500 troops and they had the mill secured within 20 minutes. In mid-November, the union conceded.

ABOVE: 'Soc et Tuum' (1896): American college sports became remarkably competitive towards the end of the century. Influenced by Oxford and Cambridge in England, sport became a source of great prestige to academic institutions, with a blurring of the lines between professionalism and amateurism as colleges sought to recruit star athletes. Then came sponsorship: the railroads courted popularity by supporting athletic contests between Harvard and Yale in 1864. Football and baseball were taking off too, and, it is gently being suggested here, colleges began to forget what they were really there for. The phrase 'sock it to 'em' dates from the Civil War and the title is a mock-Latin version. (by Louis Dalrymple)

'A Few Things the Versatile Yellow Kid Might do for a Living' by Richard F. Outcault (c.1896): The Yellow Kid strip, 'a turn-of-the-century theater of the city, in which class and racial tensions were acted out by a mischievous group of New York kids from the wrong side of the tracks', ran from 1895 to 1898 in Joseph Pulitzer's *New York World* newspaper, but transferred to William Randolph Hearst's *New York General American* as part of a circulation war. Outcault hadn't copyrighted his cartoon, so soon both papers were running the Yellow Kid. Yellow journalism became the umbrella term applied to the output of sensationalistic newspapers.

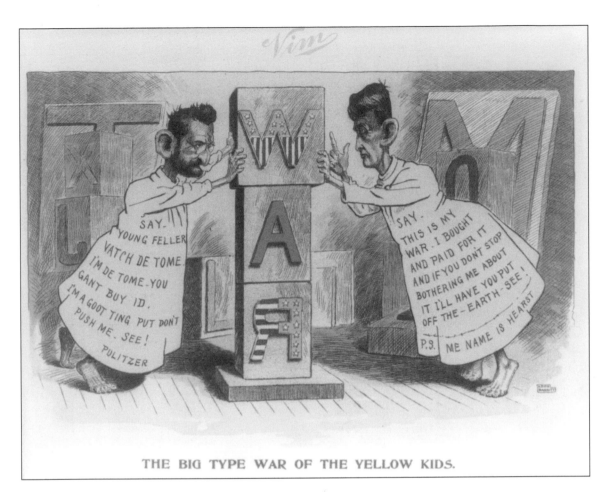

THE BIG TYPE WAR OF THE YELLOW KIDS.

ABOVE: Newspaper proprietors Joseph Pulitzer and William Randolph Hearst, both dressed as the Yellow Kid, fight to claim the Spanish–American War as their headline act and sell more papers. (by Leon Barritt, 1898)

LEFT: Grant Hamilton's satire on New York's new overhead wires and the accidents they were causing. By 1885, a mile of Broadway was illuminated by arc lights. Anyone who looked up couldn't avoid seeing dangling wires – until they were banished underground for ever by the City Fathers. That's why there are no utility poles in Manhattan to this day.

ABOVE: Thomas Nast draws a bulldog representing the New York City Police Department on Mulberry Street, leaning against a post box designed for bribes and wielding a giant billy club. In words, he further paints the picture of corruption, describing New York cops of the 19th century as the 'finest despots in the world'. (1892)

ABOVE: A daft series of vignettes by Kemble on how new-fangled electricity can help deal with door-to-door salesmen, philanderers, truants, inattentive congregations and others who stray.

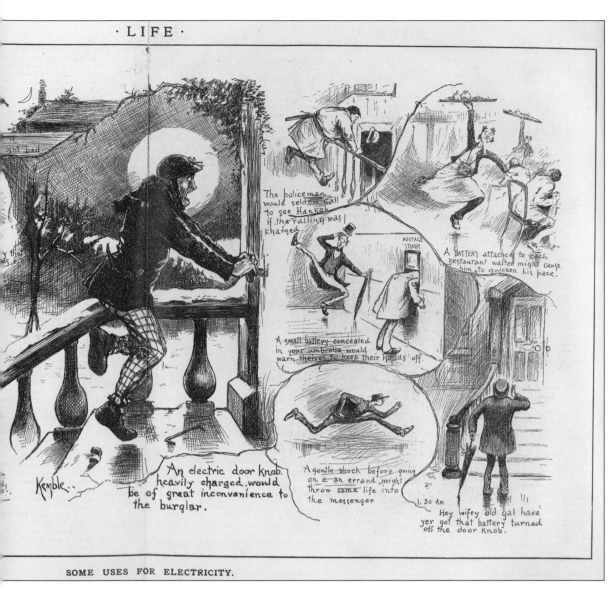

SOME USES FOR ELECTRICITY.

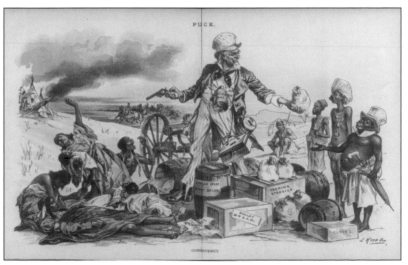

LEFT: 'Consistency' by Joseph Keppler (1891): Uncle Sam merrily hands out generous gifts to people from other parts of the world, while massacring Native Americans at Wounded Knee.

ABOVE: 'Looking Backward' by Joseph Keppler (1893): The shadows on the wall reveal what the five wealthy men were when they first arrived in America. This is a warning against placing restrictions on immigration. Immigrants have always been the lifeblood of the USA.

BELOW: 'The Great American Cow' by Tom Fleming (1896): This was the first cartoon to be entered into the *Congressional Record*. It shows Southern and Western farmers busily feeding the immense creature at one end, while the milk comes out the other into Wall Street's pail.

RIGHT: 'Lest We Forget' by Homer Davenport (c.1899): The USA emerged from war with Spain as a great world power. Inspired by Kipling's poem, 'Recessional' (1897), Davenport reminds Americans of their humble beginnings and the impermanence of power.

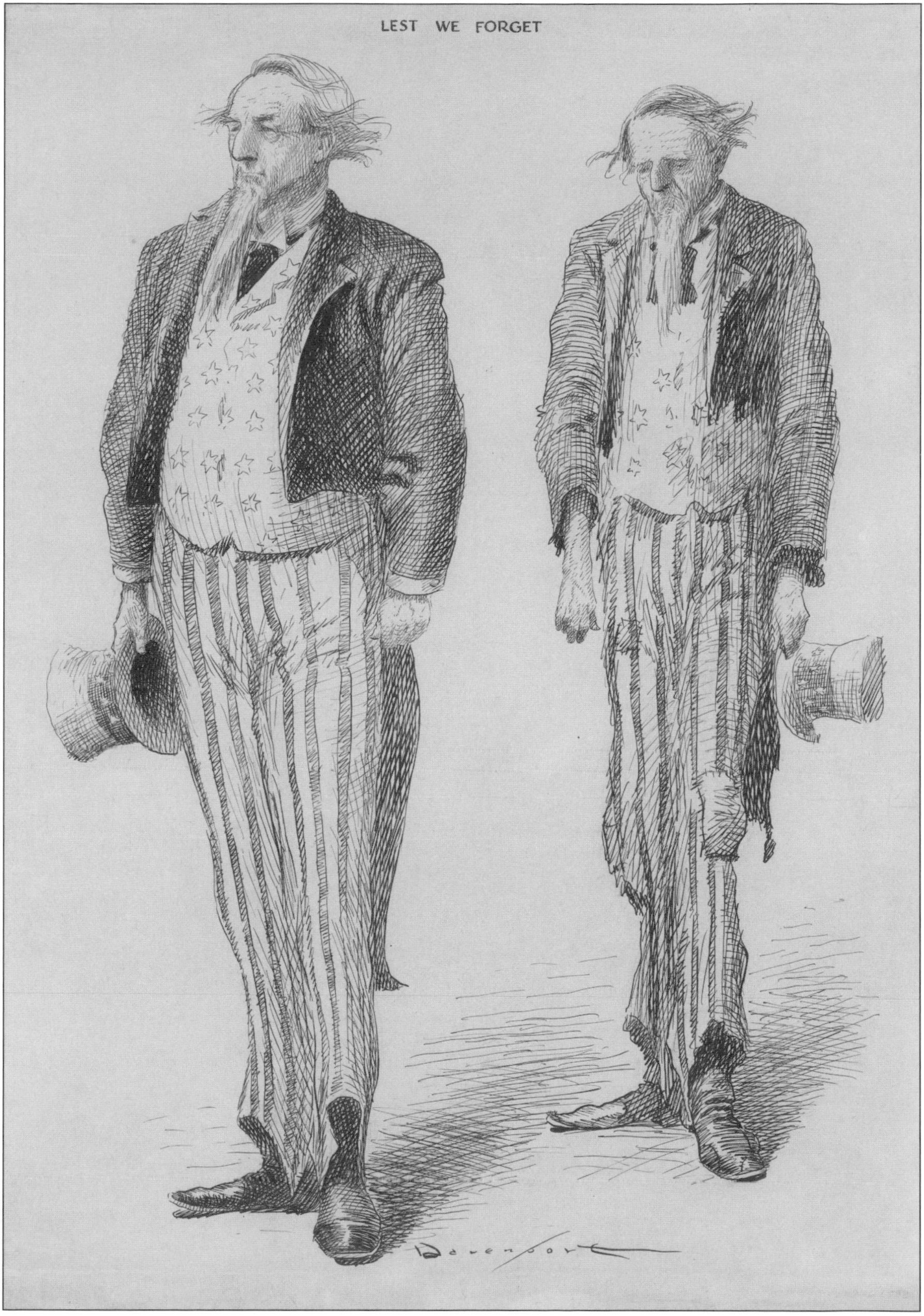
LEST WE FORGET
Davenport

Above: 'I'm Sorry I Discovered It' by Clifford Berryman (1898): In this cartoon, Spain is portrayed as a skinny, bug-eyed matador figure in tatters, running for his life from Uncle Sam's ferocious sting. This is all about Cuba which homegrown revolutionaries had been attempting to liberate from Spain since 1895. On the pretext of restoring stability, the US blockaded Cuba and then destroyed the Spanish navy, ending Spanish colonial ambitions in the western hemisphere and securing the US's future as a Pacific and Caribbean power. Spain had to cede not only Cuba but also Puerto Rico, Guam and the Philippines. America also took the opportunity to annex Hawaii.

Above: 'Only a Short Step and Uncle Sam will be in Cuba' (1894): German satirical magazine *Kladderadatsch* warns the world of American designs in the Caribbean, with the implication that the US might not stop at Cuba.

Right: McIntyre and Heath developed a 'blackface tramp duo minstrel act' which proved remarkably durable in Vaudeville and on Broadway. Reprehensible as it may seem today, they had a great influence on films stars to come such as Al Jolson.

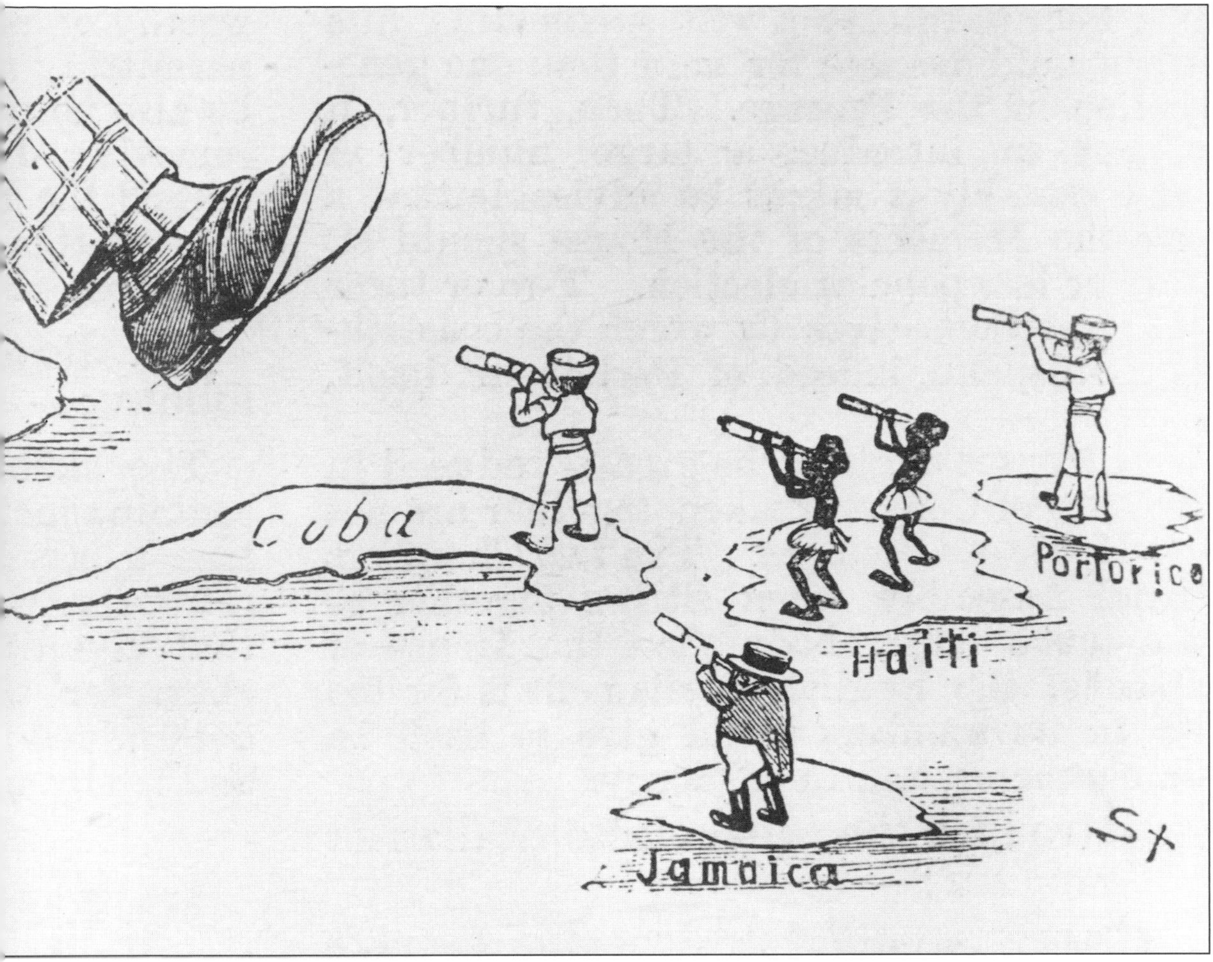
Cuba
Portorico
Haiti
Jamaica
Sx

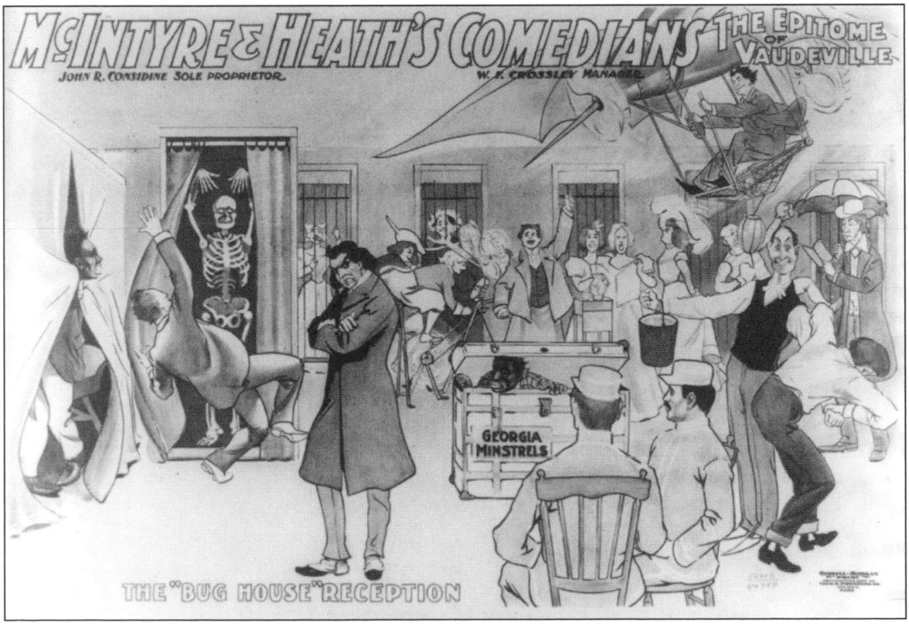
McINTYRE & HEATH'S COMEDIANS
THE EPITOME OF VAUDEVILLE
JOHN R. CONSIDINE SOLE PROPRIETOR
W. F. CROSSLEY MANAGER
GEORGIA MINSTRELS
THE "BUG HOUSE" RECEPTION

RIGHT: The Torch of Liberty has been snuffed out in this cartoon from 1895, which rails against the Blue Laws prohibiting the sale of alcohol and groceries on Sundays. The Blue Laws were first enforced by Puritans in colonial Virginia in 1610; they made church attendance compulsory, with terrible punishments for failing to comply. Sunday was reserved for worship. In the early 17th century, the celebration of Christmas was banned in certain Puritan outposts for being too frivolous. The Blue Laws, which continue to enforce religious standards, were so named because, it is thought, they were originally written down on blue paper.

The statue of Liberty (?) in her new dress.

NEW YORK UNDER THE BLUE LAWS.

" DANCE HIGHER — DANCE FASTER."

ABOVE: Frederic Sackrider Remington was a popular American
painter, sculptor, illustrator and writer who specialized in
recreating the Old American West at the end of the 19th century.
His stock in trade tended to be images of cowboys, Native
Americans and the US Cavalry. Here, a naive clerkish type rolls
into town to be confronted by a dust-stained, ornery cowpoke.

THE GREATEST DEPARTMENT STORE ON EARTH;—AND EVERY DAY A BARGAIN DAY.

LEFT: 'The Final of the American Handicap, 25 Febr.' (1897): Three men play billiards while others watch. Billiards is thought to have been brought over to the US by Dutch and English settlers. It was popularized when Michael Phelan brought out an influential book on the subject in 1850. Eventually it evolved into Eight-Ball Pool after 1900 and Straight Pool (1910). 'Pool' comes from the name for a 'collective bet or ante'.

LEFT: 'The greatest department store on earth – and every day a bargain day' by John S. Pughe (1899): Other countries are falling over themselves to buy goods from Uncle Sam, the great entrepreneur. America has become a great trading nation and Uncle Sam's customers all leave the premises happy with what they have bought.

BELOW: 'Roosevelt's idea of reorganization' (1899): Cartoon which shows Vice President Roosevelt grinding the police force into paste with mortar and pestle. Roosevelt attempted to drive corruption out of the NYPD with great reforming zeal, walking officers' beats himself, early in the morning and late at night, to check that officers were on duty.

This illustration from *Frank Leslie's Illustrated Newspaper* shows businessmen gathering in Wall Street to celebrate the dedication of the Statue of Liberty in 1886 with the first ticker tape parade. Ticker tape was normally used for transmitting financial data.

Image of the United States being swallowed whole by a huge alligator monster labeled 'MONOPOLY' and watched with concern by 'THE PUBLIC EYE'. But maybe America itself was the monster which was about to take over and dominate the rest of the world in the 20th century…

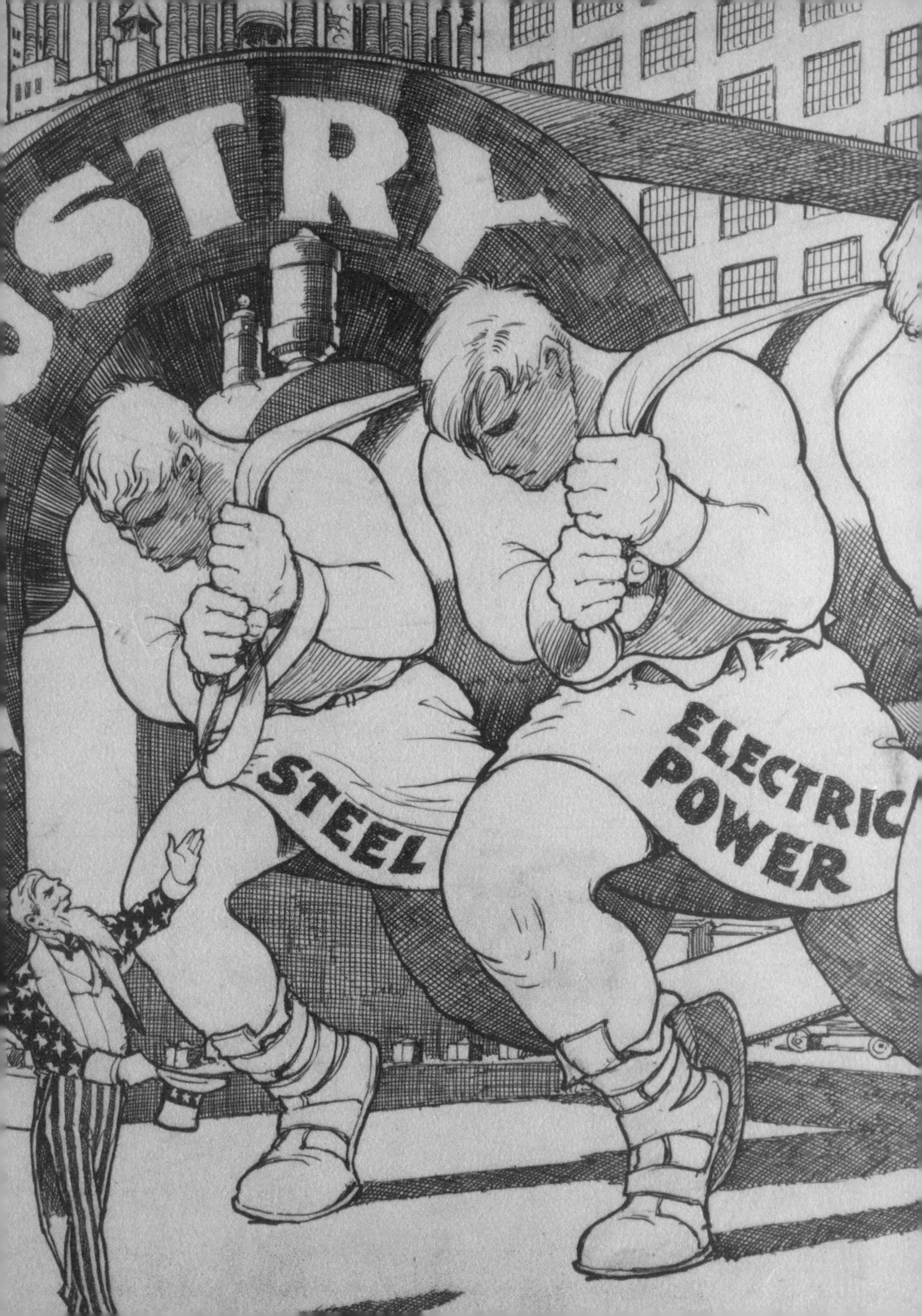
STRY
STEEL
ELECTRIC
POWER

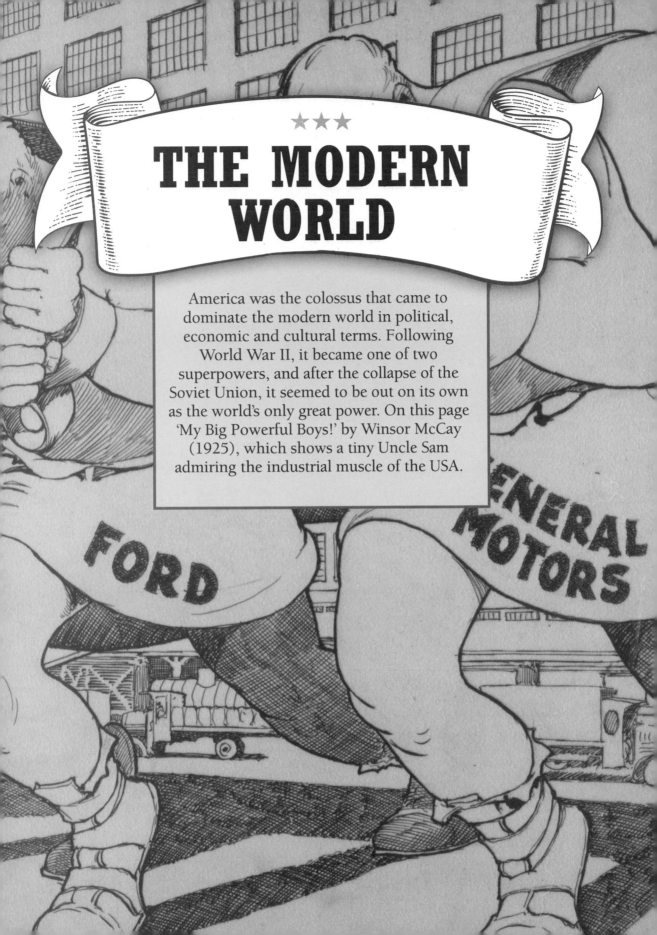

THE MODERN WORLD

★★★

America was the colossus that came to dominate the modern world in political, economic and cultural terms. Following World War II, it became one of two superpowers, and after the collapse of the Soviet Union, it seemed to be out on its own as the world's only great power. On this page 'My Big Powerful Boys!' by Winsor McCay (1925), which shows a tiny Uncle Sam admiring the industrial muscle of the USA.

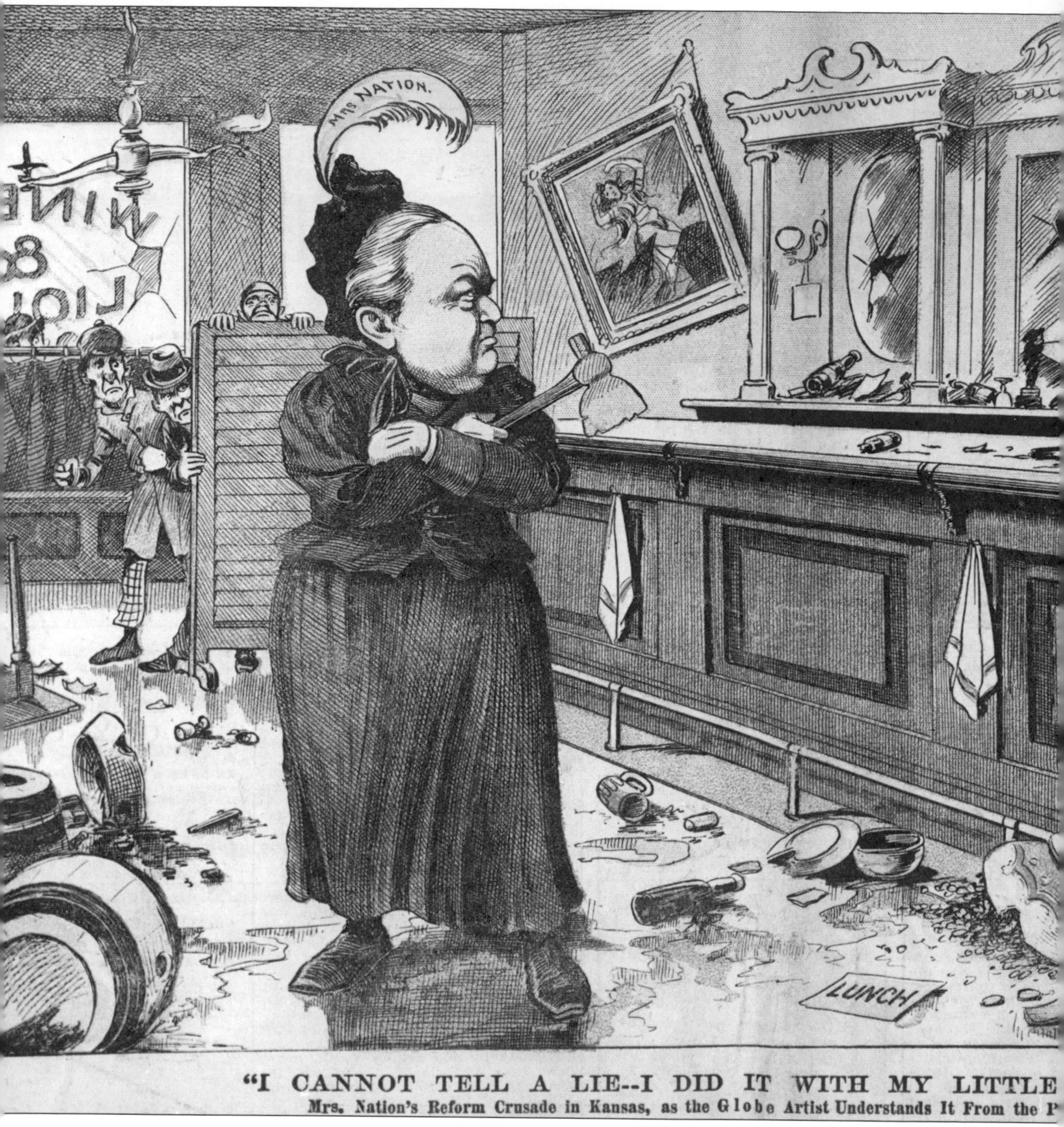
MRS NATION.
LUNCH
"I CANNOT TELL A LIE--I DID IT WITH MY LITTLE
Mrs. Nation's Reform Crusade in Kansas, as the Globe Artist Understands It From the P

Carry Nation was a temperance campaigner with a difference. She was six foot tall and nearly 175 pounds of avenging fury. Telling her hymn-singing colleagues to 'Smash, ladies, smash', she marched into bars, singing, praying and hurling biblical epithets, before smashing up the fixtures and stock with her hatchet. Nation was arrested over 30 times between 1900 and 1910 and often jailed, but she paid off fines from lucrative lecture fees and the sale of souvenir hatchets. It's said that world famous prizefighter John L. Sullivan hid in the cellar when she raided his saloon in New York City. (1901 – the quote is a reference to George Washington)

HET!"
hes.

THE KING OF THE COMBINATIONS.

John D. Rockefeller owned Standard Oil and here he seems to be willing the viewer to take him on in this inimitable image from John S. Pughe (1901). Rockefeller is wearing a huge crown adorned with all the railroads that he has 'in his pocket'. Standard Oil was so big that he could drive down the prices he paid to transport oil, or buy his own railroad companies if that suited him better, or even put them out of business if they didn't do as he said. By keeping transport prices low, he could price out the competition and then reinflate costs once rival companies had fallen by the wayside. Acquiring and absorbing other companies as part of market strategy was known as 'horizontal combination'.

"Young Corbett" and Eddie Hanlon will fight for the "featherweight" championship in San Francisco December 29. They will weigh in at 129 pounds at 6 p. m.—News Item.

Eddie Hanlon and Young Corbett square up to each other at the weigh-in for the featherweight championship in San Francisco, 1903. By most standards they were both too heavy to be featherweights. In the event it turned out to be quite a fight and was declared a draw after 20 rounds. By the end of the 1860s, boxing was staged according to the Marquess of Queensberry Rules in England. These included three-minute rounds and mandatory use of padded gloves, but they did not come into effect in America until the 1880s.

'Alice in Plunderland' by Fred Opper (1903): Another anti-Trust (anti-corporation) cartoon from a William Randolph Hearst newspaper, in which the usual suspects are going about their nefarious business(es) like bizarre automatons, observed from behind a tree by a representative of the common people. Hearst had nearly 30 newspapers in the US at the height of his power and was the model for Orson Welles' Citizen Kane.

Backed up by Secretary of State John Hay, Teddy Roosevelt
arrives in Panama to engage in a spot of 'gunboat diplomacy' –
the US offered Colombia a lump sum of $10m and $250,000
annuity to grant it exclusive rights over the Panama Canal
Zone. (Charles Green Bush, *New York World*, 1903)

HE YIELDS HIS SUPREMACY

Cartoon which records the sinking of the excursion steamer, *General Slocum*, in the East River, New York in June 1904. The vessel caught fire and sank. She was ferrying members of the St Mark's Evangelical Lutheran Church (Germans from Little Germany on Manhattan) to a church picnic. It's thought that 1,021 out of the 1,342 people on board died, which made it the worst disaster in terms of loss of life in New York City until the 9/11 attacks in 2001.

A sideways look at the Great San Francisco earthquake of 1906, showing America nursing a sore head after such extensive damage to the city and the US economy. The quake measured 7.9 on the Richter scale and resulted in the loss of 3,000 lives and 300,000 buildings. Vesuvius erupted that year too.

"AND PURSUE WITH EAGERNESS THE PHANTOMS OF HOPE."—
Sam Johnson.

In Harrison Cady's loving evocation of quackery, fadism and fakery in 1909, men and women sample all kinds of patent medicines, weight loss drinks, beauty treatments and cures for this and that. It makes you think nothing has changed. We're just as likely today to chase after Samuel Johnson's phantoms of hope.

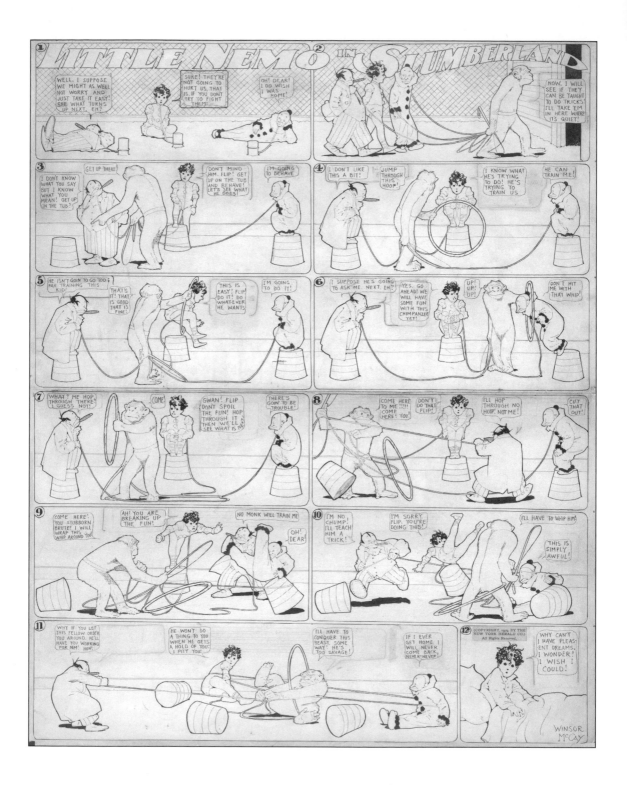

'Little Nemo' by Winsor McCay was a hugely popular comic strip that appeared in the *New York Daily Record* in 1905. Each strip is a dream which Nemo wakes from in the final panel. Beautifully drawn in an Art Nouveau style, the images had an otherworldly, surrealistic quality. McCay believed dreams reveal the secrets we hide in daily life and his cartoons provided an early entry point into the subconscious. *Nemo* means 'nobody' in Latin.

WILSON'S SUGGESTION FOR A CARTOON

CON - TROL US A — GAIN !

"If I were a cartoonist I would draw a picture of the biggest monopolies of the United States, drawn up in line and in front Mr. Roosevelt trying to lead them in a hallelujah chorus."—*Woodrow Wilson.*

—Ireland in Columbus Dispatch

ABOVE: For much of the 20th century, cartoonists were stars of the newspapers they worked on. They commanded huge salaries and were the subject of bidding wars between rival proprietors. Winsor McCay was a major celebrity of his time – his marital difficulties made the gossip columns – and, showing off his drawing skills, he appeared in Vaudeville on the same bill as W. C. Fields and Harry Houdini.

LEFT: Many cartoons of the early 20th century challenged corporate capitalism, or Trusts, in the USA. This one by Billy Ireland (1912) shows Theodore Roosevelt leading a chorus of Fat Cats singing 'Control us again' at the suggestion of Woodrow Wilson.

Copyright, 1902, by Life Publishing Co.

Theodore: I THINK I'LL WALK.

ABOVE: A fine piece of drawing by William Walker (1902) which has reluctant Teddy Roosevelt (one of the most lampooned figures of all time) riding with a massively rich man atop an elephant labeled 'GOP' ('grand old party'). Cuba and high tariffs are this creature's ball-and chains. Ominously, they have to cross a flimsy bridge marked 'Anti-Trust Sentiment' to get to Washington.

LEFT: Haunting image (c.1913) by Winsor McCay of ghostlike children powering a waterwheel, which stands as his critique of child labor. Things were slowly improving, however. By 1913, all but nine states had fixed 14 as the minimum age for factory work.

1615

1915

THE BIBLE

FASHION MAGAZINE

A·B·WALKER

THE SUBMARINES.

A LOOMING TRAGEDY OF THE POLITICAL DEEP.

Above: Alanson Burton Walker was a very popular cartoonist, whose work captured the preoccupations of his age in gently humorous fashion. With his usual fluid lines, here he compares a prim and proper Puritan woman with her counterpart, the liberated lady, 300 years later.

Left: 'The Submarines; a tragic possibility of the political deep' by Luther Daniels Bradley (1906): Two submarines in the shape of the parties they each represent have sunk to the bottom of the sea. They're both lost and there's no sign of anyone coming to rescue them.

This Cartoon shows that I
can make a "Clever One"
when I have the proper
subject.
C. K. Berryman
1913

Clifford Berryman caricatures himself in this picture (1913),
which shows him drawing a doll of President Woodrow Wilson,
while puppets of Teddy Roosevelt, William Taft and William
Bryan await his attention. Berryman's 'signature' was the Teddy
Bear. In 1902, he drew a cartoon of a hunting Roosevelt sparing
a small bear, which inspired a New York store owner to invent
the Teddy Bear, or so the story goes…

THE LETTER OF THE LAW.

ABOVE: A lithograph by Samuel D. Ehrhart (1912), which shows the smug owner of a garment factory where freezing winds sweep through wide open windows. He's telling a respectable visitor, 'That's all right! You see, we put a label on our goods guaranteeing that they weren't made in a sweat-shop.'

RIGHT: 'Together they built America' by Herbert Johnson (no date): Johnson worked for the *Saturday Evening Post* and was a strong Republican supporter. Here he puts private capitalism, democratic government, and political and economic freedom aboard a covered wagon in the form of an all-American family crossing the continent fueled by the pioneering spirit.

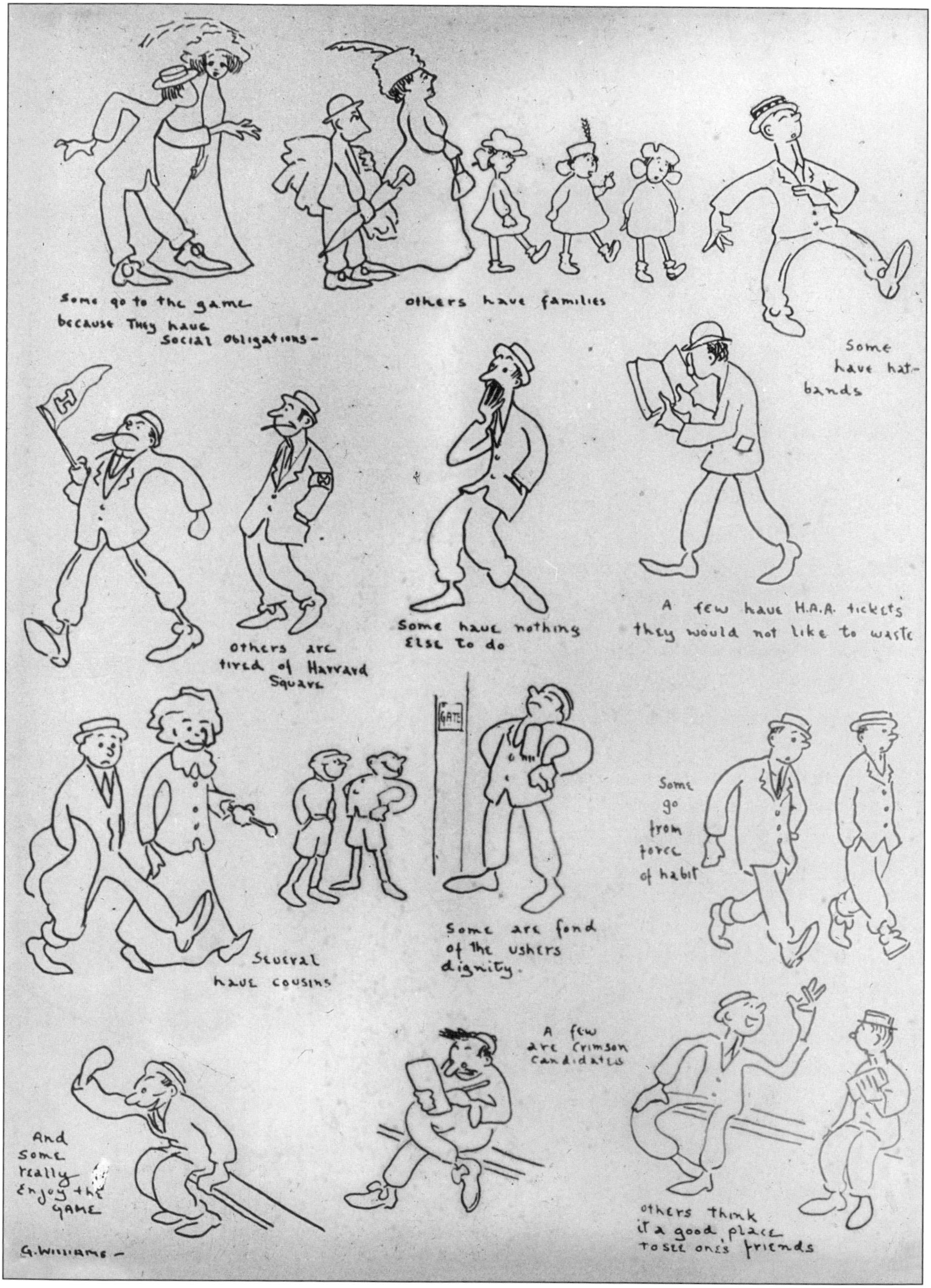

Some go to the game
because They have
social obligations -
others have families
Some
have hat-
bands
others are
tired of Harvard
Square
Some have nothing
else to do
A few have H.A.A. tickets
they would not like to waste
GATE
Several
have cousins
Some are fond
of the ushers
dignity.
Some
go
from
force
of habit
A few
are Crimson
candidates
And
some
really
Enjoy the
GAME
others think
it a good place
to see one's friends
G. Williams -

Left: 'Harvard University Football' by G. Williams (1905): These images make the game look distinctly civilized, but in 1905 there were 18 deaths during the college football season. Teddy Roosevelt invited representatives of Harvard, Princeton and Yale to the White House with a view to reducing 'the element of brutality in play'. In 1906 they brought in new regulations to minimize on-field injuries and slowly they began to turn it into the sport we know today.

Below: '12 Great Men in History: How many have you got?' by Thomas E. Powers (1912): A bingo board of caricatures of real and imagined personalities, including Theodore Roosevelt as Bwana Tombo, John Rockefeller as Oily John and a baffling, androgynous spindle labeled 'Major Joy'.

DR COOK.
INVENTOR OF THE NORTH POLE

HERMAN METZ. WHO DISCOVERED BROOKLYN

PROFESSOR GLOOM-BAYSIDE

COL DILL PICKLE CHAMPION PINOCHLE PLAYER

J SARGEANT GRAM PUBLIC SERVICE COM.

DOCTOR MARY WALKER

BILL STAM DISCOVERER OF STAMFORD

MAJOR JOY

BWANA TOM BO – 3RD TERM KID

OILY JOHN INVENTOR OF THE SOFT PEDAL.

CASEY

COL BAUM MAN WHO DISCOVERED HAIR RESTORER

ABOVE: 'Looking backward' by Laura E. Foster (c.1912): A woman forsakes her home, love, marriage and the possibility of children for a career, flattery, strife, suffrage, anxiety and loneliness on her way to 'fame'. The issue was independence and the idea of women choosing a career over the home was anathema to this artist.

RIGHT: 'The Sky is her Limit' (1920): This cartoon takes a completely different attitude to the question of women's emancipation, arguing that equal suffrage will lead to a ladder of opportunities; women will be able to throw off the yoke of domestic drudgery. This seems to be the model more widely recognized today.

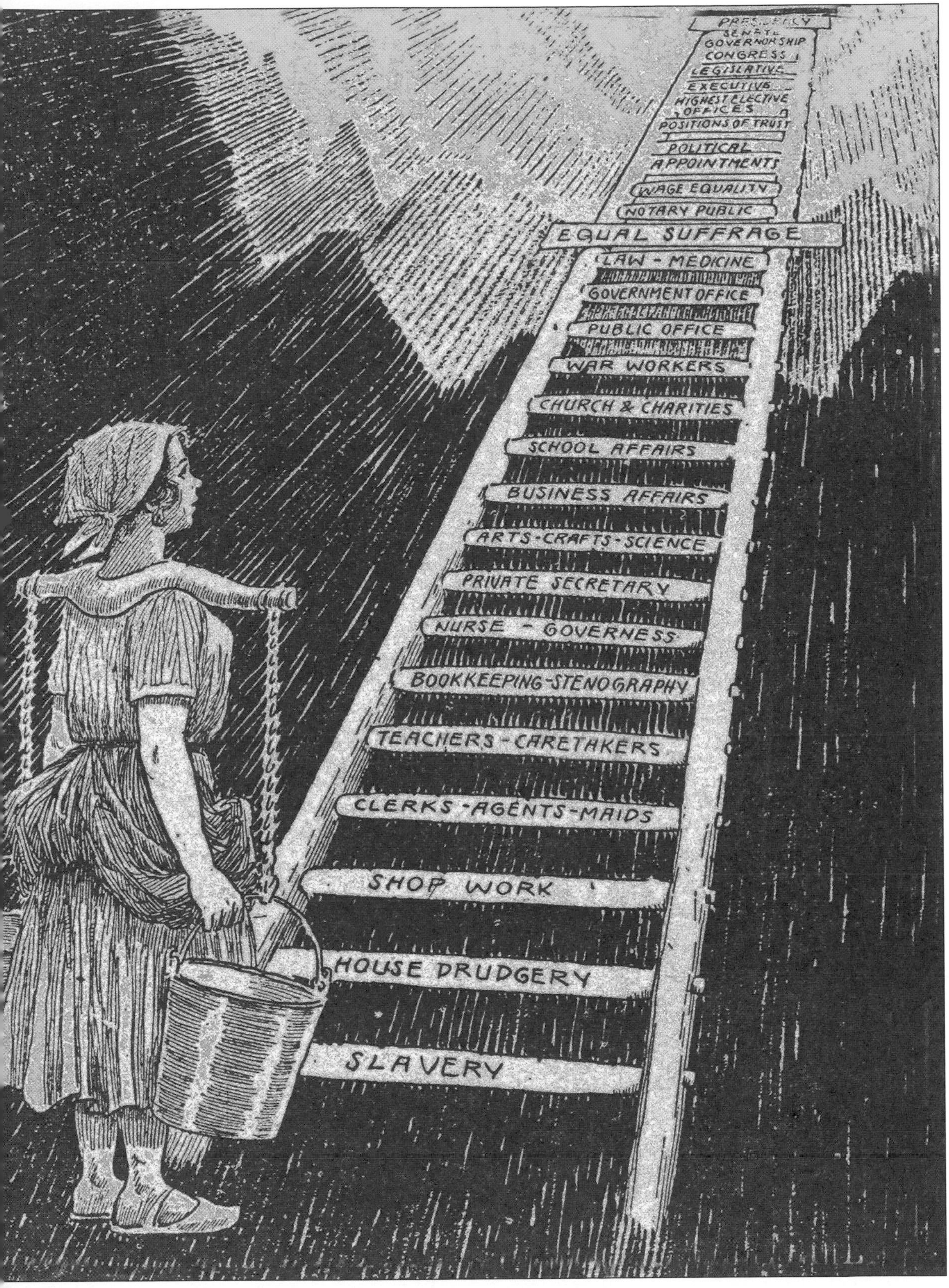
SENATE
GOVERNORSHIP
CONGRESS
LEGISLATIVE
EXECUTIVE
HIGHEST ELECTIVE OFFICES
POSITIONS OF TRUST
POLITICAL APPOINTMENTS
WAGE EQUALITY
NOTARY PUBLIC
EQUAL SUFFRAGE
LAW - MEDICINE
GOVERNMENT OFFICE
PUBLIC OFFICE
WAR WORKERS
CHURCH & CHARITIES
SCHOOL AFFAIRS
BUSINESS AFFAIRS
ARTS - CRAFTS - SCIENCE
PRIVATE SECRETARY
NURSE - GOVERNESS
BOOKKEEPING - STENOGRAPHY
TEACHERS - CARETAKERS
CLERKS - AGENTS - MAIDS
SHOP WORK
HOUSE DRUDGERY
SLAVERY

'Everybody's doing it!' by Thomas E. Powers (1912): Inspired
by Irving Berlin's dance song of 1911, this cartoon features an
all-singing, all-dancing theater stage occupied by bent politicians
and political types. A chorus line of big businessmen are kicking
a dog (the Sherman Anti-Trust Act) against a wall despite William
Taft's entreaties; Roosevelt's top hat has just been flattened by a
steamroller; and a huge pig representing the Packers' Trust presides
over a banquet of 12 jurors. They're all up to no good.

Cartoon by Louis M. Glackens (1916) satirizing the craze for ukuleles and all things Hawaiian. Tin Pan Alley was knocking out Hawaii-themed songs by the dozen and citizens of New York barely had to be asked to jump into a grass skirt and strum a ukulele. 'Ukulele' translates as 'jumping flea'.

ABOVE: 'Clubs we do not care to join – club for the retired sons of indulgent fathers' by Rea Irvin (1914): Exhausted young men mope around a splendid, spacious club with every facility laid on. Irvin worked for the original *Life* magazine, a humorous weekly. He was known as 'a truly modern bon vivant' and sophisticate about town who sought to capture and reflect the metropolitan life. Later his drawings were to set the mood and tone for the *New Yorker*.

AN ANTI-SUFFRAGE VIEWPOINT

GAYLORD (in cafe dansant): There's my wife! And I'll bet she's looking for me!
FAIR COMPANION: Oh, dear! Why can't some people understand that woman's place is in the home?

DRAWN BY W. E. HILL

ABOVE: 'An Anti-Suffrage Viewpoint' by W. E. Hill (1915): During a New Year's party, a man spots his wife and fears she will find him with his goodtime girl.

BELOW: 'In the White House Attic, a Find' by Luther Bradley (1916): Woodrow Wilson rummages through Teddy Roosevelt's old trunk and finds the famous 'Big Stick'. (Roosevelt believed in the old African adage, 'Speak softly and carry a big stick.')

BELOW: Three-time Pulitzer Prize-winning cartoonist Rollin Kirby mocks proposals by the New York State Legislature to remove restrictions on the hours women were allowed to work. Kirby was a supporter of women's suffrage, who wanted to end intolerable working conditions such as the 72-hour week and child labor.

"Until Women Vote," by Rollin Kirby, from a 1915 issue of Woman's Journal.

ABOVE: The Presidential Race of 1916 as drawn by McKee Barclay. The two-a-penny Republican vehicle is driven by the bearded Charles Evan Hughes, presidential candidate, with his potential Vice President Charles Fairbanks riding shotgun. Their automobile is labeled 'G.O.P. Promises' and its radiator is leaking ice water. At the wheel of the infinitely superior Democratic vehicle is Woodrow Wilson, with his potential VP Thomas R. Marshall in attendance as Uncle Sam prepares to fire the starting pistol. Wilson won, so perhaps Barclay had a point.

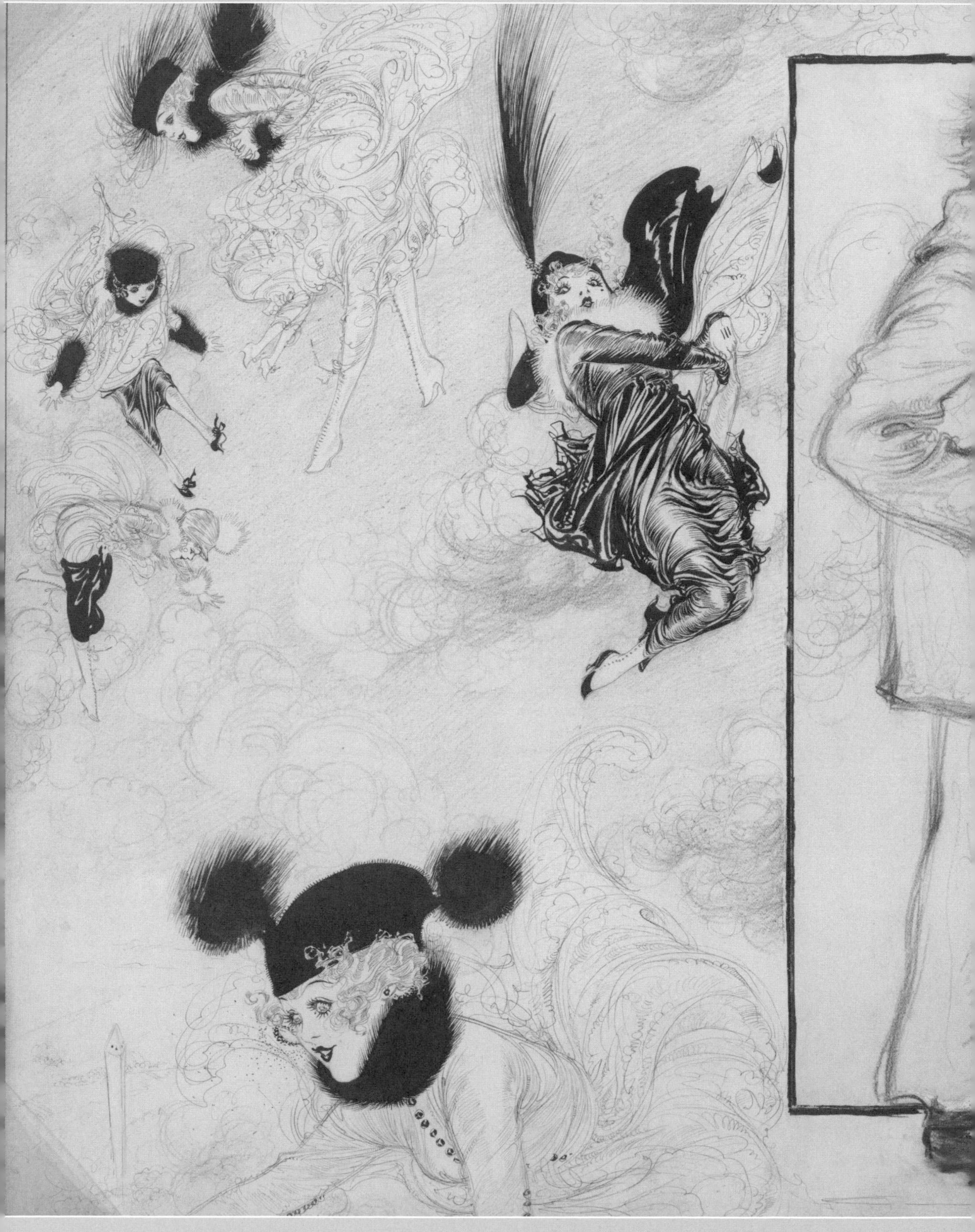

World War I

On 6 April 1917, the USA abandoned neutrality and declared war on the German Empire. Over the next two years, it mobilized around four million military personnel, of whom 110,000 died – a figure which included 43,000 victims of the terrible flu pandemic of 1918. The cartoon on this spread is 'Uncle Sam's Girl Shower' by Nell Brinkley (1918). It shows girls floating down from the sky eager to offer their services for wartime work in Washington where they encounter a housing shortage, with many landlords refusing to rent to them.

APARTMENTS
NO
DOGS
CHILDREN
OR
GIRLS

PRESIDENT
WILSON

PRIVATE

JINGO

THE AMERICAN WAR-DOG

(The American-German crisis, January–March, 1916)

LEFT: Disturbed by the howling of a dog called Jingo, Woodrow Wilson peers from the door of the White House. Swedish artist Oscar Cesare, who exhibited at the famous Armory Show in 1913, the first-ever modern art exhibition in America, wanted to encourage Americans to remain neutral in this image from 1916. In 1922 he was invited to Moscow to sketch Lenin and Trotsky.

ABOVE: A lifeboat carrying innocent victims from the Cunard Ocean Liner RMS *Lusitania* drops down into Davy Jones' Locker in this dramatic cartoon by W. A. Rogers (1915). The *Lusitania* was sunk off the coast of Ireland by German submarines in 1915, with a death toll of 1,198, including 128 US citizens. A public relations disaster for Germany, this event played a decisive role in persuading the USA to enter World War I on the side of the Allies.

'The Liberty Loan at Every Man's Door' by Charles Dana Gibson (1917): World War I happened well before the days of electronic mass media, and so it fell to popular artists, who 'rallied to the colors', to supply the images that moved the masses. Journalist George Creel was in charge of the Committee of Public Information, the body in charge of drumming up posters for the war effort. He also persuaded celebrities such as Charlie Chaplin to make speeches promoting war loans.

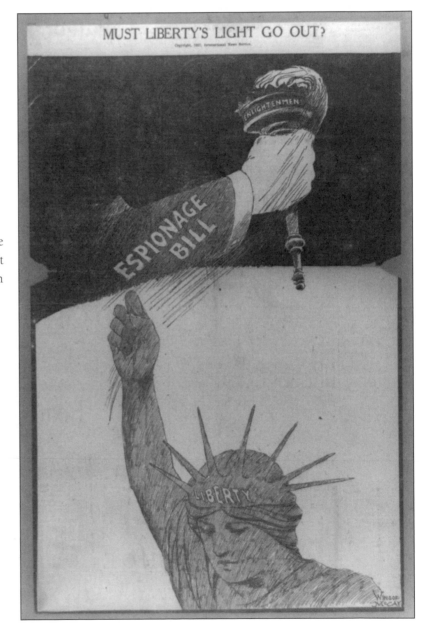

MUST LIBERTY'S LIGHT GO OUT?

'Must Liberty's Light Go Out?' by Winsor McCay (1917): The Espionage Act of 1917 made it a crime to 'convey information intended to interfere with the war effort or to promote the success of the nation's enemies'. In reality, it came to be used against socialists and anti-war protestors. Later, the act was dusted off after the war for use during the first 'Red Scare', a time when fear of communism in the wake of the Russian Revolution reached its height. This fear was exacerbated by militant union activity and a series of anarchist bombings. The Espionage Act is still used against government 'leakers', including Edward Snowden.

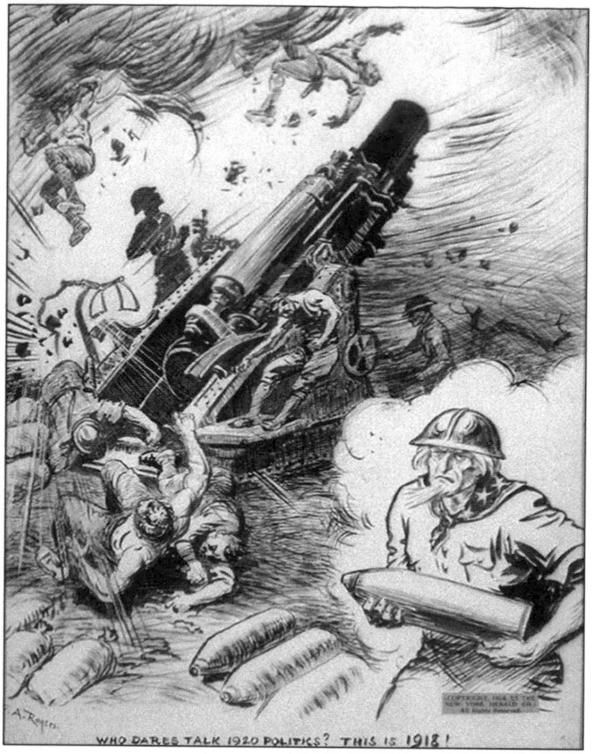
WHO DARES TALK 1920 POLITICS? THIS IS 1918!

Left: 'Who Dares Talk 1920 Politics? This is 1918' by W. A. Rogers (1918): As shells explode all around him, Uncle Sam rolls up his sleeves to lend a hand on the front line in Europe. By April 1918, there were 650,000 US troops in France, with more than 10,000 arriving each day. Rogers, who was a regular cartoonist with the *New York Herald*, is saying that it is too early to talk about what to do with disaffected soldiers after the war (a hot topic of the time)... much more importantly, there was a war to be won.

Right: 'The Breath of the Hun' by W. A. Rogers (1918): The change of mood in the US is shown by this cartoon of the alien menace hovering over NYC. During WWI, the Federal Government registered around half a million alien civilians and kept them under surveillance. Over 6,000 men and women were sent to four detention camps in the US and, controversially, half a billion dollars of assets and property were confiscated to fund the war. In Hot Springs, North Carolina, detainees constructed an authentic German village, complete with its own church made out of tobacco tins.

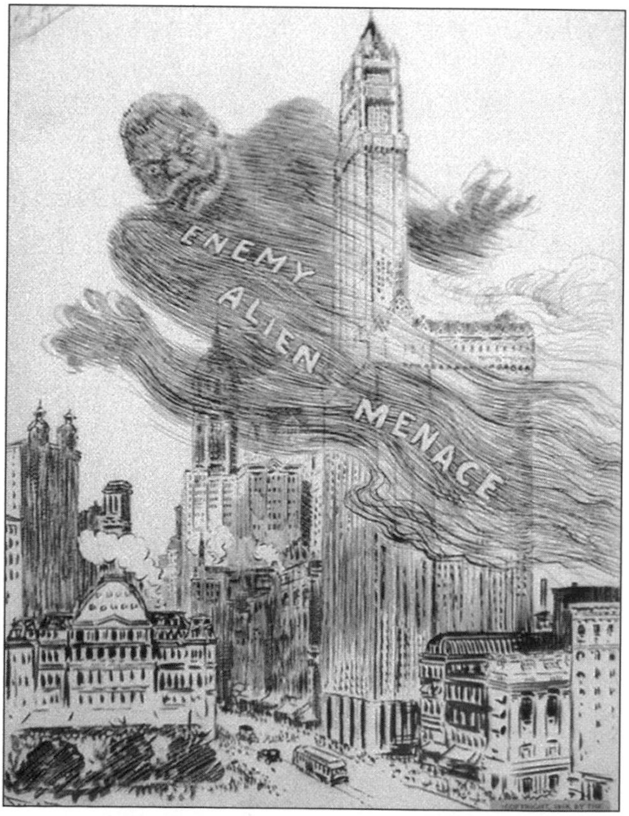
ENEMY ALIEN MENACE

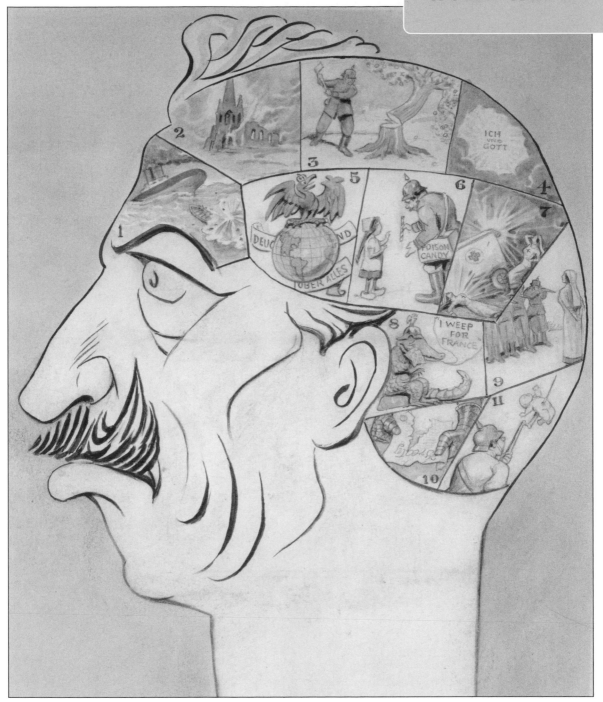

'Frenzylogical Chart' by Oliver Herford (1917): Readers of *Life*, where this image was published, would have been familiar with the way that phrenologists had divided up the human brain. For example, Area 1 was Humanity and shows the sinking of the *Lusitania*; 3 is Love of Nature and shows a soldier chopping down a tree; 6 is Generosity and we see a Dutch girl being given poisoned candy. This cross-section of 'the German mind' is like a tick sheet of the success of Britain's long-running, anti-German propaganda.

ABOVE: 'The Limit' by W. A. Rogers (1918): Another anti-alien image which shows a large German, or perhaps a citizen of the Austro-Hungarian Empire, sitting next to Uncle Sam and taking up more than his fair share of the bench in Liberty Park as a snake heads menacingly toward a snail.

RIGHT: 'Votes for Women Bandwagon' by Clifford Berryman (May, 1919): Politicians climb aboard the bandwagon as it heads for Congress. On 4 June 1919, the 19th Amendment (female suffrage) passed both houses of Congress and was ratified by sufficient states in 1920. WWI played a big part in helping women gain the right to vote, since so many had given their all, working outside the home, to the war effort.

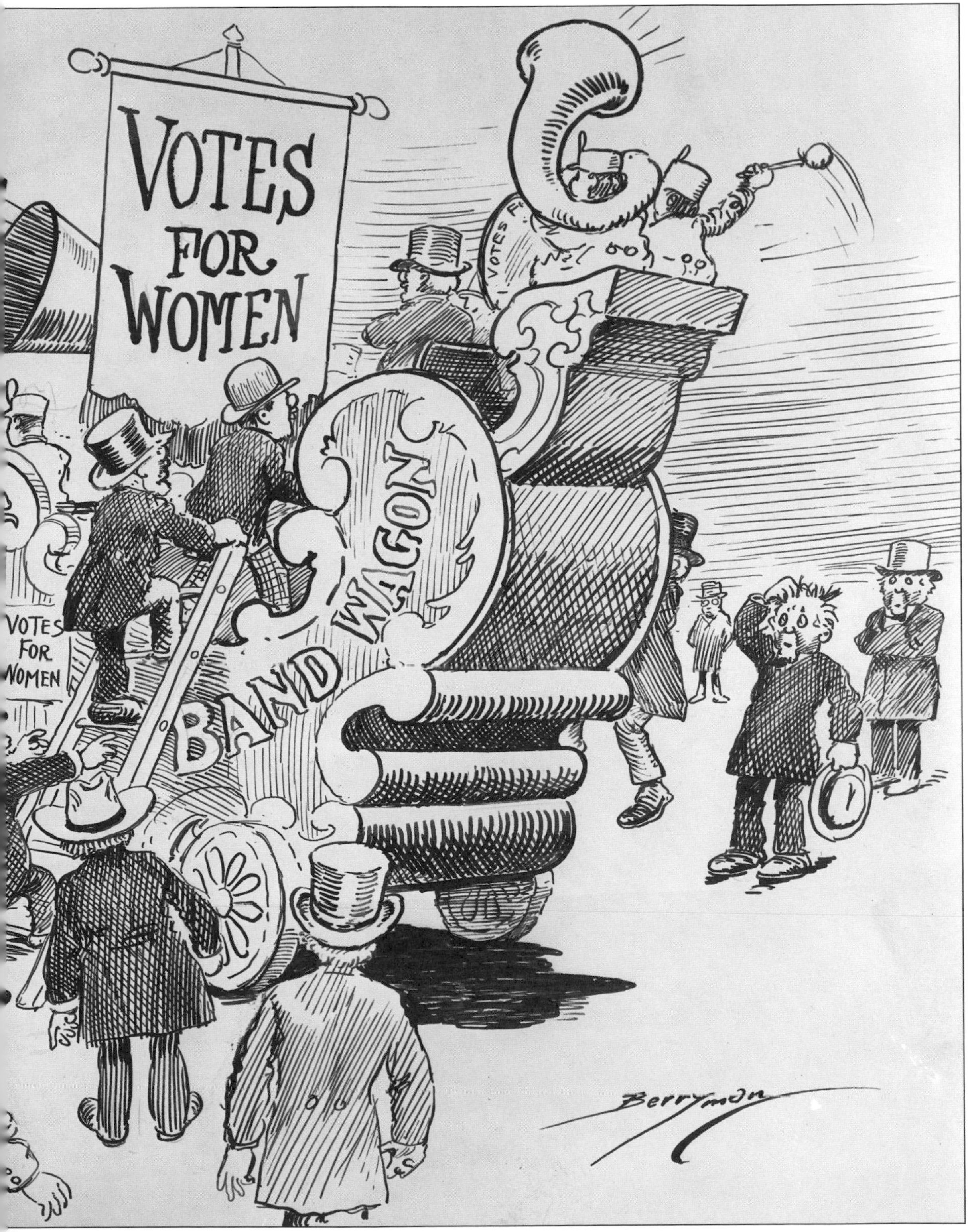
VOTES FOR WOMEN
BAND WAGON
VOTES FOR WOMEN
Berryman

ABOVE: '"Their" Playground' by Clifford Berryman (1922): Gloomy kids watch cars go by at speed and wonder where they are going to play now that the wasteground where they played in Grant Circle, Washington DC, has been taken from them. The automobile was taking over. In 1922 there were around 7.5 million cars in the US and they were changing the American landscape. The introduction of Henry Ford's Model T, a car affectionately known as 'Tin Lizzie', started the revolution in 1908. It was the world's first 'affordable automobile'.

LEFT: In an experiment to see whether airplanes could be used effectively against shipping, the German battleship *Ostfriesland*, which had been captured in WWI, was sunk by the bombs of US Army planes off the Virginia Capes in June 1921. It was a sitting duck. (by John T. McCutcheon, 1921)

BELOW: 'Masked Criminal at the Grave of John Barleycorn' by Ralph Barton (1921): 'John Barleycorn' is an old English folk song and the personification of whiskey and beer. Barton is making the point that liquor was often presumed to be the cause of crime, but it wasn't until alcohol was banned under Prohibition that crime ran rampant. The criminal, incidentally, is firing his gun at a fleeing Pilgrim…

Betty Boop was one of the world's most popular cartoon characters in the 1930s. She first appeared in 1930 as a Jazz Age flapper with more heart than brains. Betty was unique among female cartoon characters because she was sexualized, her every move suggestive. She became a symbol of the Depression Era. Under the Production Code of 1934 (part of the Hays Code), she had to tone down her act. She became a housewife or career girl in a fuller dress and was never quite the same again.

'In a Sea of Reel Trouble' by Cy Hungerford (1922): Hungerford heralds the arrival of Will Hays as President of the Motion Producers and Distributors of America in 1922. Answering growing calls for censorship, Hays was supposed to 'clean up the pictures' and save Hollywood from itself following such scandals as the alleged rape of aspiring actress Virginia Rappe by the famous comic film star Roscoe 'Fatty' Arbuckle.

LES ENFANTS TERRIBLES
JOHN DOS PASSOS and F. SCOTT FITZGERALD

Cartoonist Gene Markey knew everybody in
Hollywood. He was an author, producer and
screenwriter and he married three famous film
stars, Joan Bennett, Hedy Lamarr and Myrna Loy.
The image above was produced for a book called
Literary Lights (1923). F. Scott Fitzgerald, chronicler
of the Jazz Age, was a frequent subject of caricature;
John Dos Passos wrote the *USA* trilogy which is
considered one of the great works of American
literature. They're both pictured as spoilt brats,
but they probably found that quite amusing. Who
knows?

'Hollywood – the Talkies Science. The problem of the permanence of the human voice on a plate – "Alas, poor posterity, can you ever forgive me? I've gone and made the Hamlet eternal."' by Will Dyson (1929): *The Jazz Singer*, the first feature-length talkie, came out in 1927 and doomed silent movies to the dustbin of history. Some were briefly resurrected with post-dubbed dialogue and songs.

FIVE MONTHS AGO

THE OAK

DAYTON

THIS IS THE LIFE!

DAYTON

TO·DAY

THE OAK

EVOLUTION IN TENNESSEE

Fueled by the oxygen of publicity, a mountain man from Dayton, Tennessee evolves into a man mountain in a big old suit basking in the limelight. This cartoon alludes to the case of John T. Scopes, who in July 1925 was tried for violating a Tennessee state law prohibiting the teaching of Evolution in public schools. He was defended by lawyer Clarence Darrow and the courtroom in Dayton was besieged by the media, Christian fundamentalists, and the simply curious. Scopes lost the case and was fined $100, but his conviction was later overturned. (by Clifford Berryman, 1925)

In 1922, a competition was held to find a design for the *Chicago Tribune* Tower; the first prize was $50,000 (equivalent to $700,000 now) and entries poured in from renowned architects across the world. Cartoonists were also asked to submit their designs, which included this drawing for a skyscraper by Frank King, based on Uncle Walt in his popular 'Gasoline Alley' strip.

THE SANTA FÉ TRAIL

Cartoon saluting the pioneering spirit of Army pilots John A. Macready and Oakley G. Kelly in making the first non-stop transcontinental flight across America (by Rollin Kirby, 1923): Macready and Kelly flew their single-engine, high-wing Army Fokker T-2 over 2,625 miles from Mitchell Field, New York to Rockwell Field, San Diego, a coast-to-coast journey that took 26 hours, 50 minutes, 48 seconds, with a mid-flight engine repair thrown in for good measure.

LEFT: 'Wonders of the Wireless Age' by John T. McCutcheon: The first radio broadcasts took place in America in 1922 and by 1930 60 percent of households had radios. It became the must-have entertainment center of the age – people held dance parties round the glowing dial and radio shows of all kinds became ingrained in American culture. Sounds that came out of the ether seemed deeply magical to many people of the time, none more so than to the man on this page who believes his radio can do anything.

BELOW: Pulitzer Prize-winning cartoonist Clifford Berryman produced a 'Spring Cleaning Days' series. Here, we see the father of the house reduced to the status of outcast as a cyclone of activity takes place behind him and clouds of dust fly. (1925)

The non-stop baby needs new shoes.

They've just become engaged, and where there's no sense there's no feeling.

THE DANCING MARATHON

"The first hundred hours are the hardest"

Sketches by Johan Bull

The gentleman seems to have lost the spirit of the thing.

The hours I spend with thee, dear heart, are but a string of blisters.

What a difference just a few hours make! The light fantastic grows a trifle heavy.

The odds are against him.

ABOVE: Out of such zany 1920s enthusiasms as Flagpole Sitting and Six-Day Bicycle Races emerged the giddy Jazz Age fad of Endurance Dancing. Couples had to remain in motion for 45 minutes every hour but, if your knees touched the floor, you were disqualified. Come the Depression, some dancers were just too desperate for prize money and dance marathons were no longer fun.

RIGHT: 'Yes, Sir, He's my Baby' by C. H. Sykes (1927-8): President Calvin Coolidge plays the sax for a flapper wildly dancing the Charleston. Free marketeer Coolidge famously said, 'The business of America is business.' Actually, he didn't say much else, being laconic to the point of near-silence. When he died in 1933, wit Dorothy Parker remarked, 'Calvin Coolidge dead? How can they tell?'

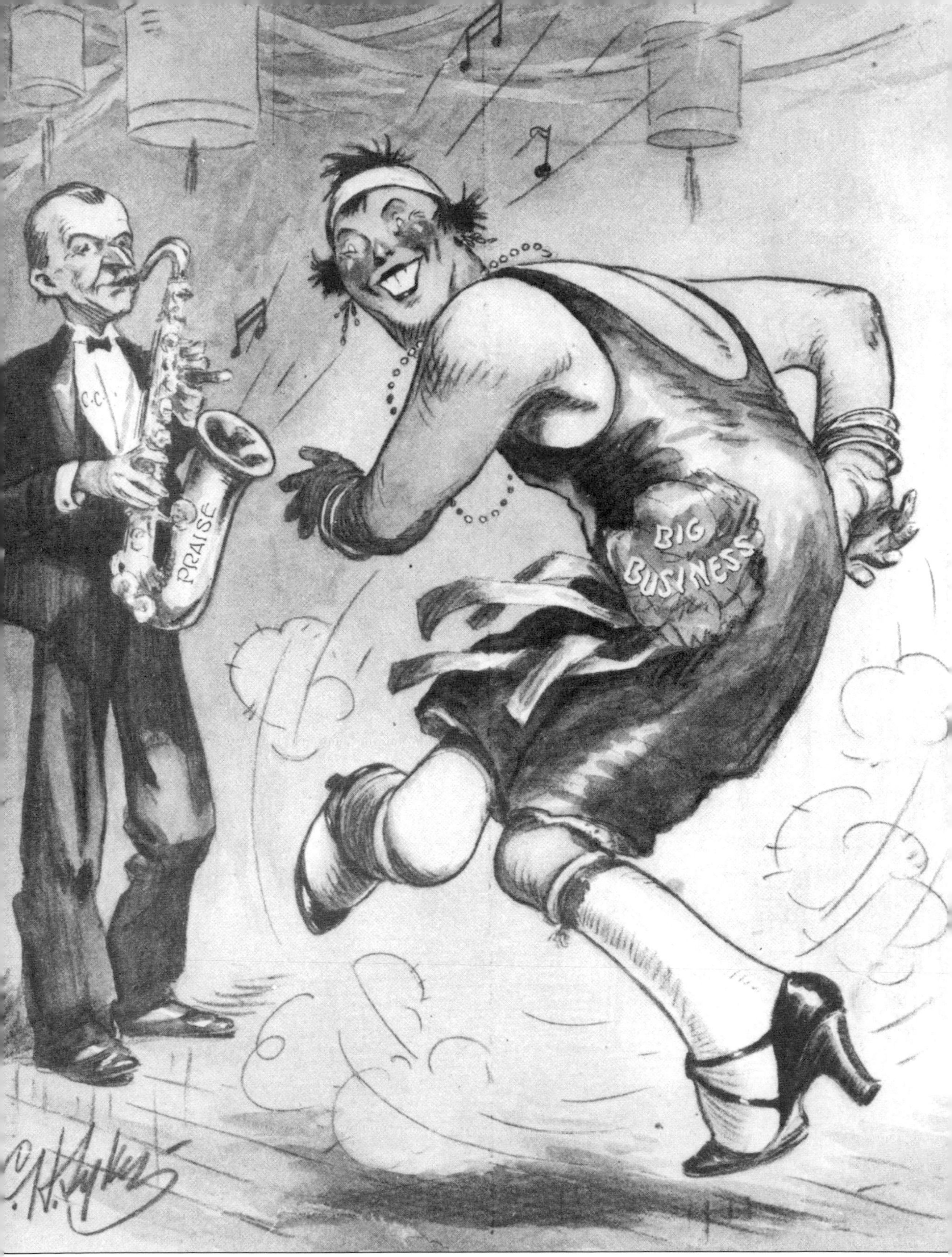
C.C.
PRAISE
BIG BUSINESS

'I Want to Make their Flesh Creep' by Rollin Kirby (1924): The Republican Party 'Fat Boy' shakes a straw dummy labeled 'Red Scare' into life, the artist's comment on the anti-Red hysteria that swept the USA after WWI. Right-wing politicians kept whipping the frenzy up again and again.

THE TIN GOD.

A businessman looks up to see a shining vision that means money (by D. R. Fitzpatrick, 1927): Henry Ford had developed the assembly line and conveyor belt, leading to cars being built more and more quickly. Ford's River Rouge plant in Detroit was the biggest factory in the world. During the 1920s, America was spending about $1bn a year putting together a national network of highways, which was good news for everyone. The success of the automobile led to a huge expansion of the economy. No one thought about pollution.

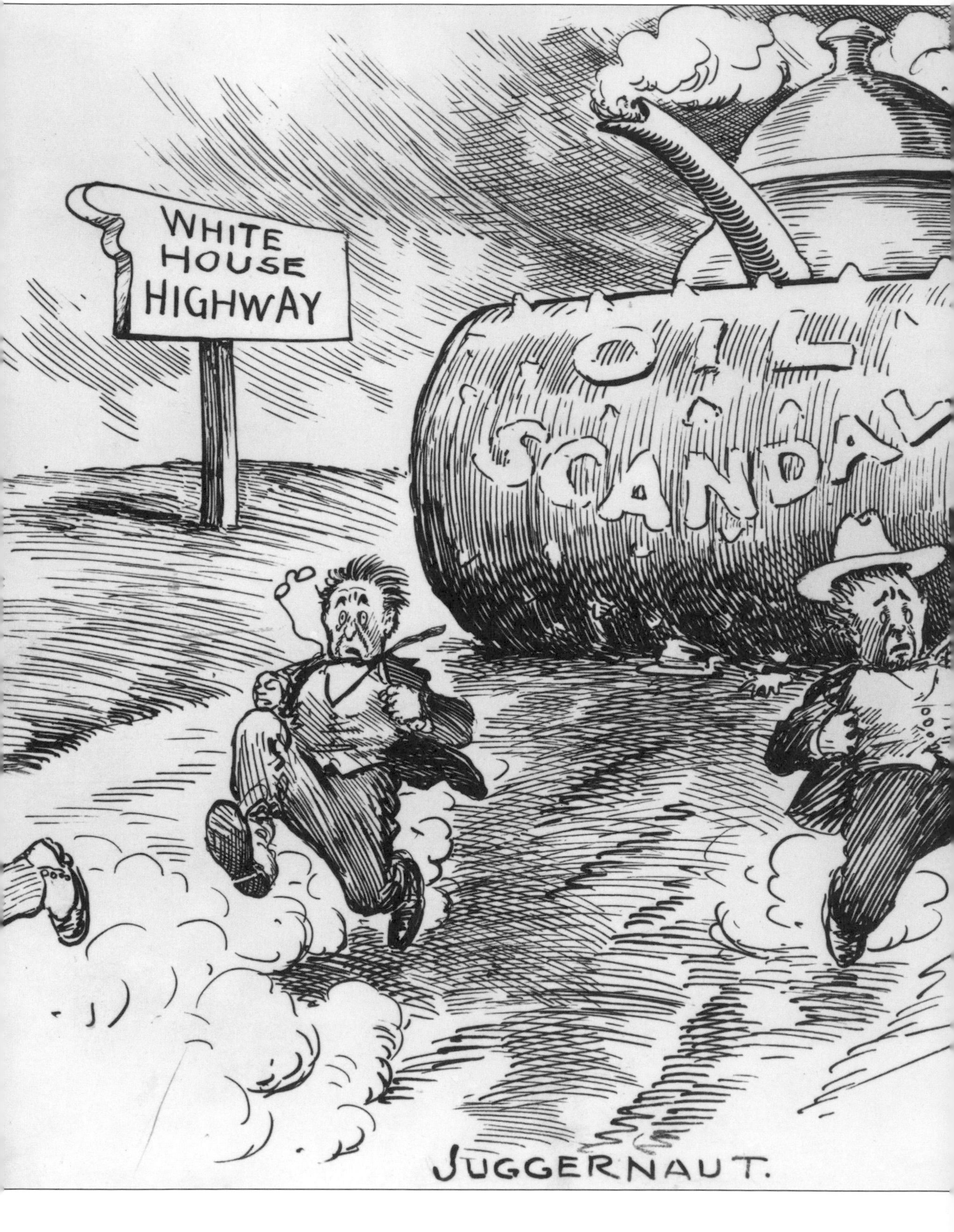
WHITE HOUSE HIGHWAY
OIL SCANDAL
JUGGERNAUT.

LEFT: The Juggernaut of Scandal heads towards the White House, leaving steamrollered politicians lying flattened in its wake (by Clifford Berryman, 1924). The Teapot Dome Scandal began when Albert B. Fall, US Secretary of the Interior, illegally leased federal oil reserves to companies in exchange for cash. One of these reserves was in Wyoming, topped off by a teapot-shaped rock. Fall was imprisoned in 1931.

ABOVE: 'Club Life in America: The Stockbrokers' by Charles Forbell (1929): The Wall Street Crash is remembered here without much sympathy as stockbrokers line up to read the ticker tapes of doom and then, assisted by servants, attempt to exit this life in an amusing variety of ways.

Inspired by the idea of labor-saving devices as a cause of unemployment, left-wing cartoonist Art Young produced this image around 1927. A pair of giant mechanical hands are pushing the workers of the world on to a massive scrap heap. Young had studied under Thomas Nast in the late 19th century and believed that cartoons could effect political change.

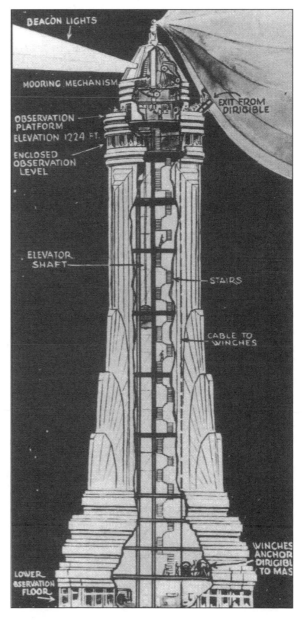

BELOW: Design for the Empire State Building, which President Hoover dedicated in 1931 by pressing a button in the White House which turned on the building's lights. At 1,250 feet high, the Empire State was the world's tallest skyscraper and a beacon of pride for Depression-era America.

BEACON LIGHTS

MOORING MECHANISM

EXIT FROM DIRIGIBLE

OBSERVATION PLATFORM ELEVATION 1224 FT.

ENCLOSED OBSERVATION LEVEL

ELEVATOR SHAFT

STAIRS

CABLE TO WINCHES

WINCHES ANCHOR DIRIGIBL TO MAS

LOWER OBSERVATION FLOOR

'Dr Common-Sense's Great Cure!' by Winsor McCay (c.1930-34): After
the stock market crash of 1929, the US economy crumbled as recession
turned into the Great Depression. By the early 1930s, more than 15 million
Americans were unemployed (a quarter of the workforce), but President
Hoover continued to argue that patience and self-reliance would see the
country through as he twiddled his thumbs. That was why Franklin Delano
Roosevelt called him the 'hear nothing, see nothing, do nothing' president.
In 1932, Roosevelt took over in the White House, bringing with him the
New Deal, a set of government policies designed to provide a safety net for
US citizens who were down on their luck. His first act was to shore up the
nation's banks. Gradually, confidence came back in line with Roosevelt's
statement that there was 'nothing to fear but fear itself'.

John Dillinger was a notorious hoodlum who blazed a trail of violence across the American Midwest in the early 1930s. He and his gang robbed banks and police arsenals, killing over ten men and staging three successful jail breaks. In 1934, he was betrayed by one of his girlfriends. When he went to see Clark Gable in *Manhattan Melodrama* at the Biograph Theater, Chicago, the feds were waiting for him when he came out. He was shot three times by FBI agents and pronounced dead in hospital a few hours later.

After the Revenue Act of 1935, America's highest earners had to pay a tax rate of 75 percent on their income over a certain amount, and Franklin D. Roosevelt was seen as the friend of the man in the street. However, the 'Roosevelt Recession' of 1937–38 led to criticism. Suddenly he just seemed power-hungry and cynical. (by Quincy Scott, 1938)

Another Myth Exploded

FDR SAYS IT IS NOT AT ALL TRUE THAT HE "HAS GRILLED MILLIONAIRE FOR BREAKFAST;" THAT WHAT HE REALLY LIKES IS SCRAMBLED EGGS.

'I AM THE LAW'   by Ellis

CONSTITUTION
BILL OF RIGHTS

MAYOR HAGUE

NEWS ITEM: Mayor Hague's Jersey City police arrest CIO organizers attempting to distribute leaflets to workers and run others out of town.

'I Am the Law' by Fred Ellis (1937): An image, perhaps influenced by Hollywood gangster movies, shows Frank Hague, Mayor of Jersey City from 1917 to 1947, lighting a cigar with the Constitution and the Bill of Rights. An astute political operator who maintained power through a mix of 'violence and benevolence', Hague held a stranglehold over politics in his home town. He was famous for his ability to 'get out the vote'. At one point, Jersey City had 147,000 residents over 21 (the legal voting age) and 160,050 on the electoral register.

Sam Goldring specialized in cheap and cheerful 1930s postcards which often bordered on the ribald and scandalous, and which captured the mood of the times for many ordinary people. Some of these cards sold in great numbers and, if you couldn't be funny yourself, Goldring was your man – he did the jokes for you!

'I overran Chicago and I Can Run Over You' by D. R. Fitzpatrick (1932): Chicago was Al Capone's kind of town back in the 1930s, with kidnappings, assassinations, extortion, protection rackets, graft and corruption a regular feature of everyday life. In 1931 Capone was sentenced to 11 years in federal prison for tax evasion but his absence didn't make much difference to the figures. Serious crime hardly let up as the decade ran its course....

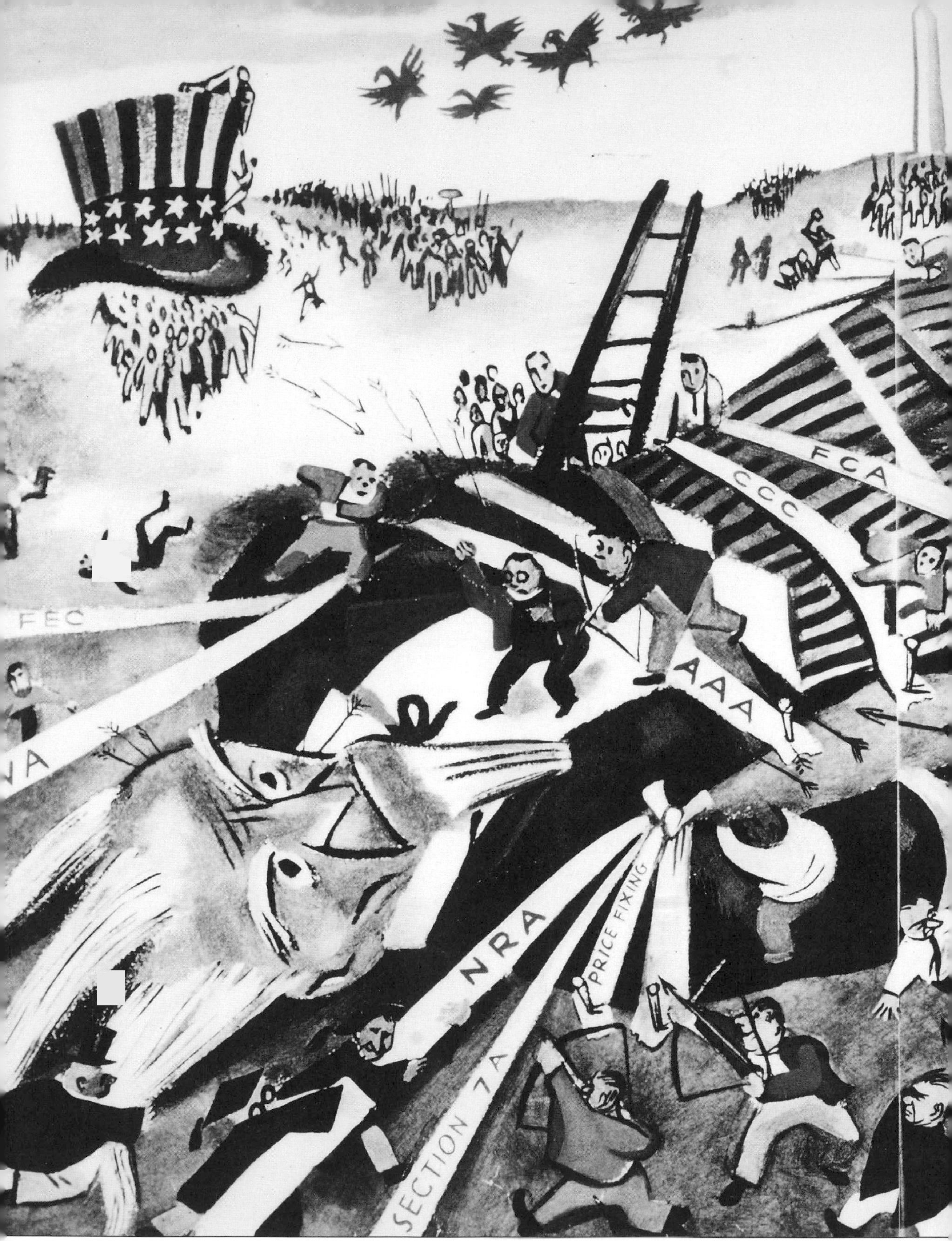
FCA
CCC
FEC
AAA
NRA
PRICE FIXING
SECTION 7A

"LAND OF THE FREE, AND HOME OF THE BRAVE"

ABOVE: When Orson Welles' *The War of the Worlds* was broadcast on the radio on 30 October 1938 it is alleged large portions of its audience – they had come in too late to hear the introduction – fled their homes believing there had been a Martian invasion, so realistic were some of the show's news announcements. This inspired Les Callan's cartoon in the *Toronto Star*, which points out that some Americans were just as susceptible to fiction as the Germans.

LEFT: New Deal cartoon by William Gropper (1935), which shows Uncle Sam tied down Gulliver-like by the 'alphabet agencies of the New Deal', largely set up to help the 'little people'. Gropper belonged to the Ashcan School of art, a body dedicated to expressing urban life and industrialization. He said, 'People create the landscape of my paintings.'

'BUT IT WOULD MAKE SUCH A NICE SCOOP IF YOU'D ONLY TELL ME, FRANKLIN.'

This is the cartoon which so amused Mrs. Franklin D. Roosevelt that she had her secretary write to The Chronicle requesting the original drawing by Burck. It originally appeared in this newspaper April 28 and is being reprinted for the benefit of those who may have missed it two weeks ago.

Professor Einstein

Low

LEFT: Eleanor Roosevelt wrote a column for a newspaper entitled 'My Day' which elicited this response from cartoonist Jason Burck. She was tickled by the idea that she'd have a scoop if her husband told her whether he'd be running for a third term. Outspoken and out there, Roosevelt was the first First Lady to create headlines all by herself.

ABOVE: Portrait of Albert Einstein by David Low which first appeared in the *New Statesman*. Because of his political stand against the Nazis and the fact that he was Jewish, Einstein left Germany and eventually went to live in the United States, taking citizenship in 1940 and teaching at Princeton.

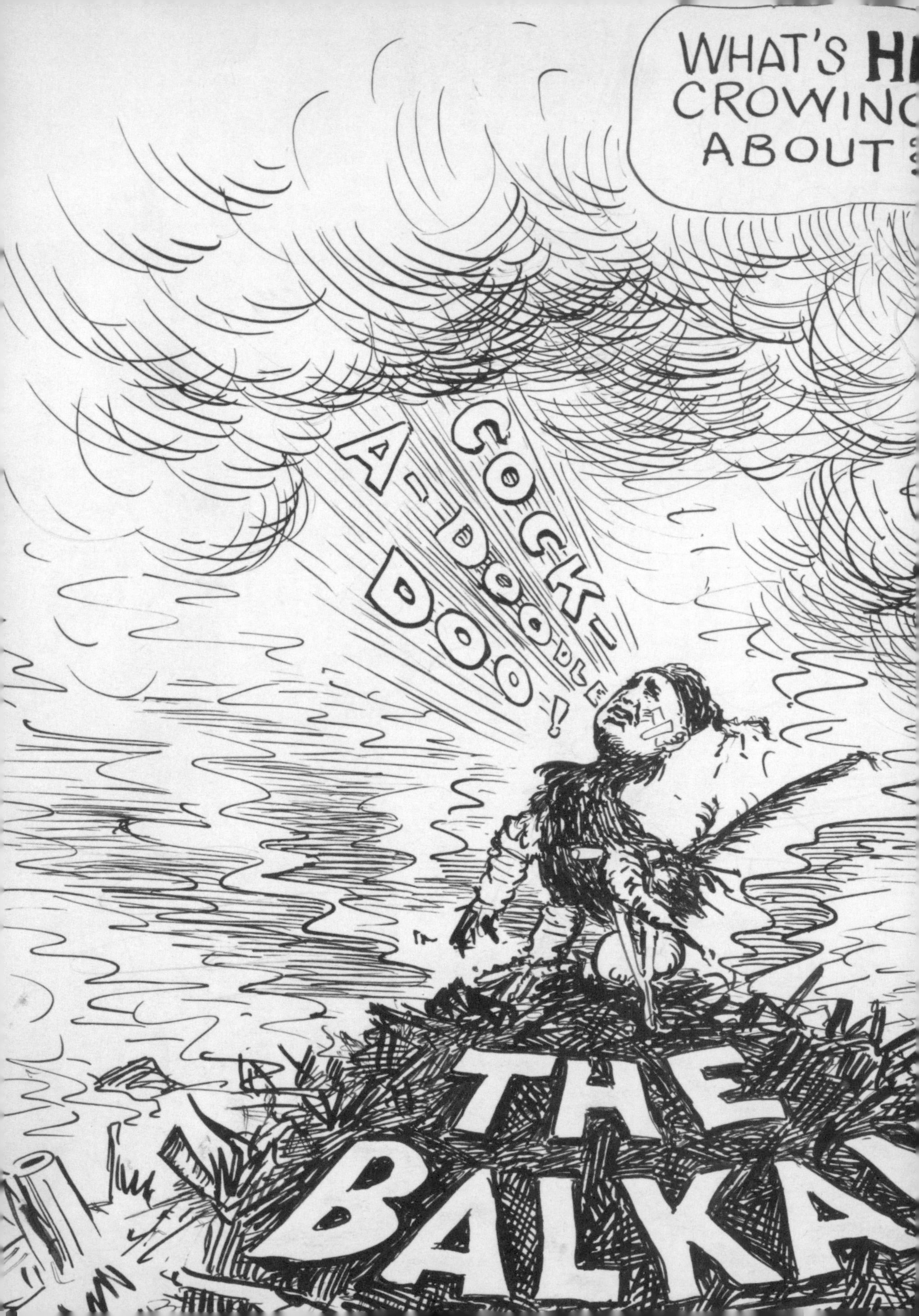
WHAT'S
CROWIN
ABOUT
COCK-A-DOODLE-DOO!
THE

World War II

It wasn't until the Japanese launched a surprise attack on Pearl Harbor on 7 December 1941 that the US was drawn into World War II. Congress declared war on Japan the very next day and the country was quickly mobilized to meet the challenge of the Axis Powers. The cartoon here shows Adolf Hitler as a vulture watching Mussolini the cockerel blowing his own trumpet in the Balkans in the spring of 1941. Mussolini was trying to claim the glory for defeating the Greeks when they had already surrendered to the Germans.

ABOVE: A three-headed snake with the faces of
Hirohito, Adolf Hitler and Benito Mussolini.
(1942)

ABOVE: American women played a big part in winning
WWII – 19,000,000 of them served in the home front
labor force. Women worked in shipyards, aircraft and
munitions factories; they drove trucks and even signed
up for the Coast Guard. In fact they took over jobs that
had previously been the sole preserve of men. (1942)

RIGHT: 'Frankenstein?' by Herb Block
(1940): Block shows an alarmed-looking
Stalin watching the German Juggernaut
lurch into life. Herb Block supported
intervention in the European war and
drew many cartoons to encourage this. US
public opinion began the war supporting an
isolationist position, but by 1941 70 percent
favored taking on the Nazis.

'All On One Hand' by Edwin Marcus (1940): Adolf Hitler is portrayed as a snake-eyed poker player staking everything on one big gamble. This image was drawn as the Germans ended the 'Phony War' and launched their Blitzkrieg on Belgium, France and the Netherlands. Marcus produced another very famous WWII cartoon showing Uncle Sam reaching in his pocket to pay for a film called *Saving Democracy* – implying it was US duty to fight Hitler.

Fresh, spirited American troops, flushed with victory, are bringing in thousands of hungry, ragged, battle-weary prisoners. (News item)

The cartoon which won 23-year-old Bill Mauldin the Pulitzer Prize. As a sergeant with the 45th Division, Mauldin landed in Sicily and worked for *Stars 'n' Stripes* magazine. He produced around six cartoons a week, providing a warts-and-all version of what life was like for regular US soldiers, known as 'dogfaces', on the front line. His work was phenomenally popular among serving men. Mauldin's attitude earned him a ticking off from General Patton, but Eisenhower said he provided a safety valve for the frustrations of GIs.

'Uncle Sam Cleaning Up the Japanese Invasion Fleet after the Battle of the Coral Sea' by Willard Combes (1942): Jolly propaganda image in which Uncle Sam is shown as Neptune picking up Japanese vessels on his trident as if they are toy boats. In reality, the battle proved to be a pyrrhic victory for the Japanese who lost too many vessels to maintain supremacy in the region.

'You're the man, Jones, who said car pooling wouldn't work!' (1943): Car pooling was encouraged to save on gas and rubber tires. Joe Public was bombarded with messages to share his car with others; one poster said, 'When you ride alone you ride with Hitler'. The one above is aimed at beguiling men into compliance.

SMOKING CHIMNEYS

FROM SMOKING GUNS TO

A neat idea from Edwin Marcus in 1945 – turn this image on its side and it goes from smoking cannons to the smoking chimneys of peace time. Marcus was being optimistic, but belching chimneys have taken on a negative meaning today…

ABOVE: Charles Henry Alston produced biographical portraits of outstanding African-Americans like this one of Joe Louis (1943), Heavyweight Champion of the World from 1937 to 1949. In 1990 his bust of Martin Luther King, Jr. became the first image of an African-American on display in the White House.

RIGHT: D. R. Fitzpatrick flies the flag for NATO, the North Atlantic Treaty Organization, which began life in 1949 as little more than a political association brought into existence by fear of the Soviet Empire. When the Korean War started, NATO began to arm itself to the teeth. Its counterpart in the East was the Warsaw Pact.

BANNER OF THE NON-SOVIET UNION

The Cold War was probably inevitable after WWII, given the competing ideologies and interests of the victors. In 1948 the Soviet Union imposed a blockade on West Berlin, which comprised the French, American and British sectors, an island of democracy deep within the Eastern Bloc. The Allies began an airlift which successfully reprovisioned the city. In 1949 the Soviets lifted the blockade. This image drawn by Fitzpatrick in 1949 captures the distrust and hysteria conjured up between the competing Superpowers, which was to last for decades.

SEN.
Mc CARTHY

RED
PAINT

ACCUSATIONS

ABOVE: Senator Joseph McCarthy started his major anti-communist drive by claiming there were 200 communist party members among the staff in the US State Department. But was he painting himself into a corner with all those smears? When McCarthy was finally discredited in 1954, he started drinking heavily and died a broken man in 1957. (by Edwin Marcus, 1950)

RIGHT: Supreme NATO commander Eisenhower stutters over the hurdles on his 1951 tour to rally western Europe. He said, 'In a world in which the power of military might is still too much respected, we are going to build for ourselves a secure wall of peace.' Watching are Stalin and his generals with their 'secret weapon' of peace, but they look more likely to invade. (by Opland for Dutch newspaper *de Volkskrant*)

Opland in Volkskrant, the Netherlands

"Hooray, Eisenhower!"

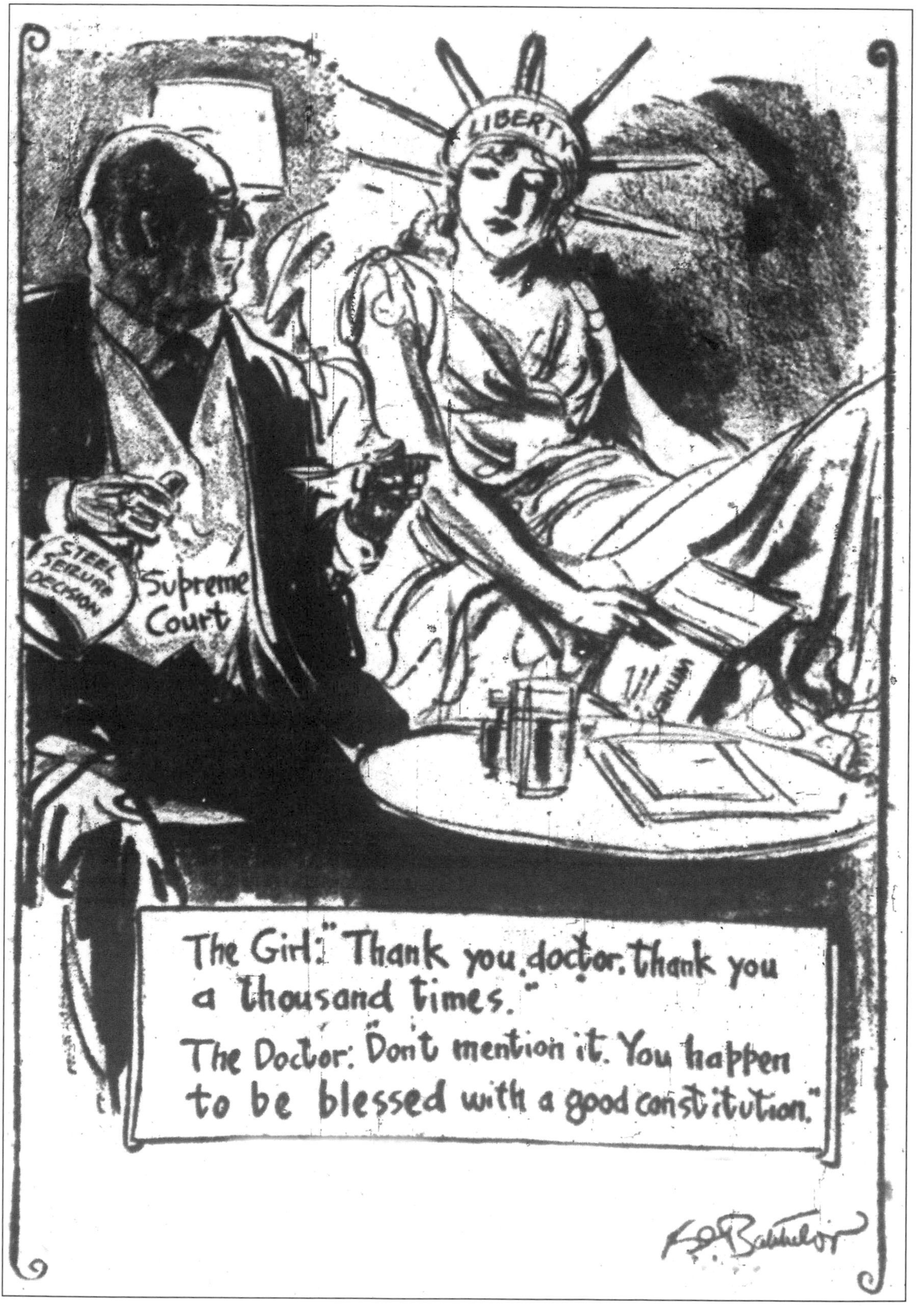
LIBERTY
STEEL SEIZURE DECISION
Supreme Court
The Girl: "Thank you, doctor. thank you a thousand times."
The Doctor: "Don't mention it. You happen to be blessed with a good constitution."

RIGHT: 'Falsies!' by Fred Packer (1952): Cartoon suggesting that the prosperity attributed by Democrats to Truman's Fair Deal policy – which sought to go beyond his predecessor Roosevelt's New Deal – was created by inflation and Korean War spending. It had no solid foundations!

LEFT: Faced by a strike of steel workers for higher pay during the Korean War, President Truman nationalized the steel industry before the workers walked out. The steel companies took their case to the Supreme Court and were given back their premises. The court ruled that Truman had no right to seize the steel mills without the backing of Congress. This cartoon shows Liberty as a woman with a good constitution. (by C. D. Batchelor, 1952)

RIGHT: Soviet soldiers race between bomb craters during the Korean War in this cartoon by Herb Block (1950). One of them is saying, 'You know, that Cold War wasn't so bad.' The Cold War was a lot less dangerous than the real thing – it could have been soldiers from either side making this observation.

A typical Cold War-era cartoon by Reg Manning (1953) which shows Molotov, Malenkov and the Russian bear looking in horror at the object they fear most, the secret ballot box, as guards hold back the crowd. 1952 marked the end of the Marshall Plan after WWII and the US was by now into a new phase, obsessed by its relations with the Soviet Bloc which were ultra-cool going on freezing.

'Easter Egg Coloring' by Edwin Marcus (1952): Joseph
Stalin uses propaganda to try to convert the world to
communism. 'Uncle Joe' made his last speech in 1952 to
the 19th Party Congress of the Communist Party of the
Soviet Union. He died in March 1953, and for quite a
period of time his servants were too scared to enter the
room where the great tyrant lay. There is still speculation
that he may have been murdered.

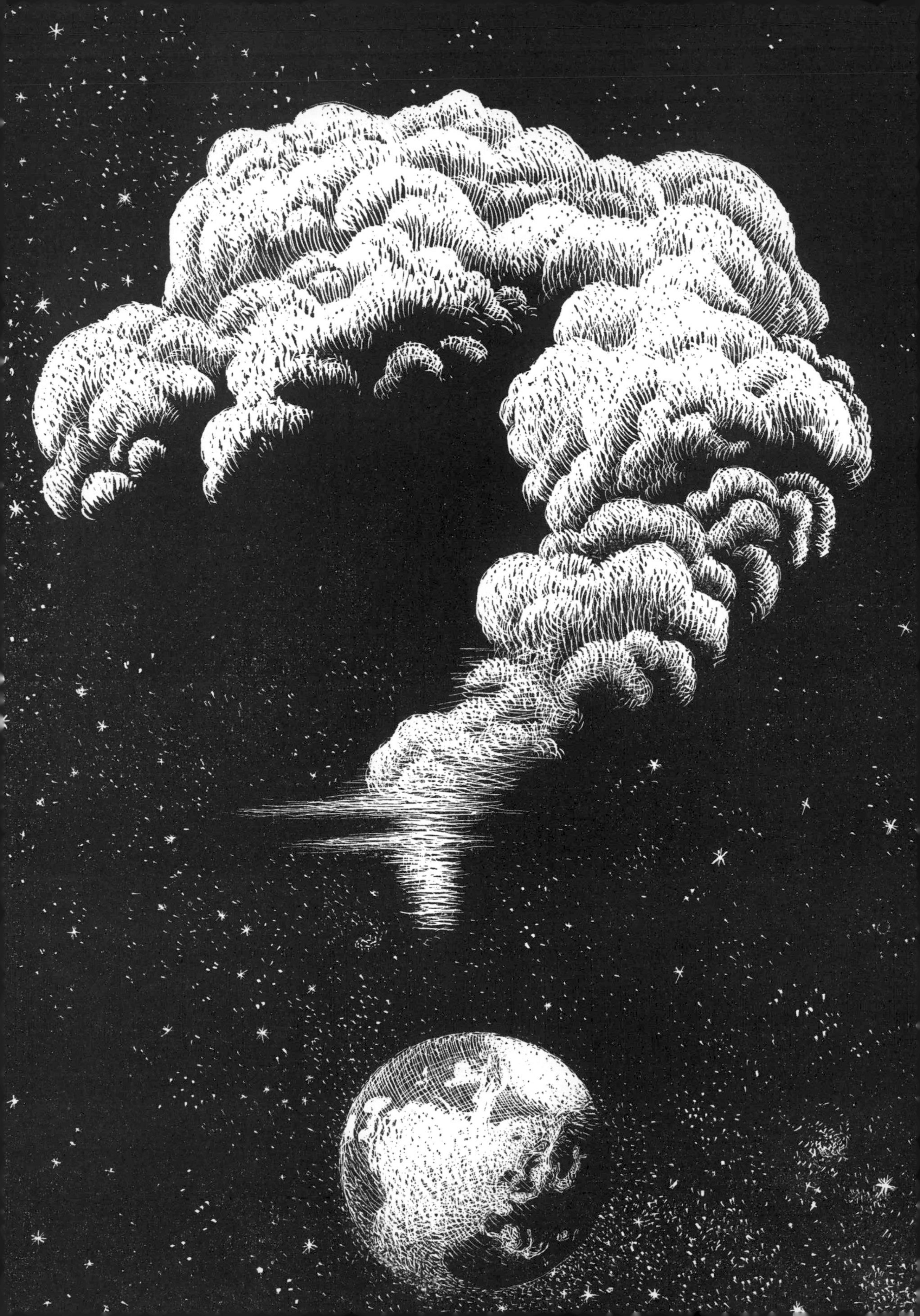

Left: Leslie Illingworth's brilliant rendering of the threat of nuclear war hanging over the world in 1954. The Soviet Union tested its first atom bomb in 1949 and panic escalated. In 1952 the US exploded the first hydrogen bomb on Bikini atoll. This bomb is reckoned to have been around 1,000 times stronger than the bomb which flattened Hiroshima. It was so powerful that the measuring instruments failed. No wonder everyone was scared.

Right: Marlon Brando brought a new intensity to acting in his Oscar-winning role as dockworker Terry Malloy in *On The Waterfront* (1954), which is about union violence and mob corruption at the docks in Hoboken, New Jersey. It's the movie where his character, an ex-boxer, says, 'I could a' been a contender.'

THE MESS IN DOWNTOWN ST. LOUIS

"WE NEED A GOOD LAUGH THESE DAYS"

LEFT: D. R. Fitzpatrick pictures St Louis grinding to a halt as a new city-county government takes over the reins of municipal control in 1954. This new government district was soon rejected by voters. Fitzpatrick worked for the *St. Louis Post-Dispatch*.

ABOVE: Two representatives of Big Business laugh at a piece of paper labeled 'Ike's Tariff Policies'. Eisenhower was in favor of a three-year extension of the tariff-cutting Reciprocal Trade Agreement which was thought to prioritize international business over domestic matters.

'59 MODELS TO BE EVEN LONGER (News Item)

Wed., May 14. 1958   ST. LOUIS POST-DISPATCH

LEFT: In the 1950s, American cars just got bigger and bigger, with extensive use of chrome and lights, space-age design and massive tailfins – some of them looked like grounded rockets. Bill Mauldin thought it was all getting out of hand and wondered how to fit them into suburban garages. The expansion of the automotive industry gave a huge boost to the US economy; by the end of the decade, at least one in six workers was employed directly or indirectly in automobiles as car ownership doubled. (1958)

"THEY WANT TO GO SLOW, CHILD. THAT'S WHAT THEY SAID 80 YEARS AGO."

Wed., June 25, 1958   ST. LOUIS POST-DISPATCH

LEFT: The US Supreme Court ruled that racial segregation in public schools was a violation of the 14th Amendment. However, resistance to desegregation grew in the South, and the 'Southern Manifesto' was launched. A court in Little Rock sought to derail integration but was overruled. Here, Bill Mauldin is making a point about how nothing much had changed in the South. (1958)

"We eat between 11.30 and 12, so we have our lunch hour free for shopping"

'Sounds like a plan to me' (1955 from *Everybody's Weekly*): Although this cartoon actually appeared in a British magazine, the look and feel are American even if the attitude, the leisurely office lunch, is strictly homegrown. Post-WWII, US culture came to dominate Europe. High-brow French gangster movies were influenced by Hollywood, almost all the major international music stars were American and, if you wanted to treat yourself, it had to be Coca-Cola you drank. At this time, lots of European performers made a career out of imitating the big names from the USA. America meant style.

"CRAZY, MAN, CRAZY!"

Mon., April 27, 1959

ST. LOUIS POST-DISPATCH

ABOVE: Beatniks look in awe at a prancing Fidel Castro. Castro took over Cuba in 1959 after ousting dictator Fulgencio Batista. Beatniks gained recognition in the late 1950s as an urban sub-species of jive-talking nonconformists who'd read Kerouac's *On the Road*.

RIGHT: Bill Mauldin shows three tiny schoolkids pushing against the weighty door of segregation which is slowly admitting light. The 1960s would be a decade when the question of Civil Rights came to the fore and progress could be made.

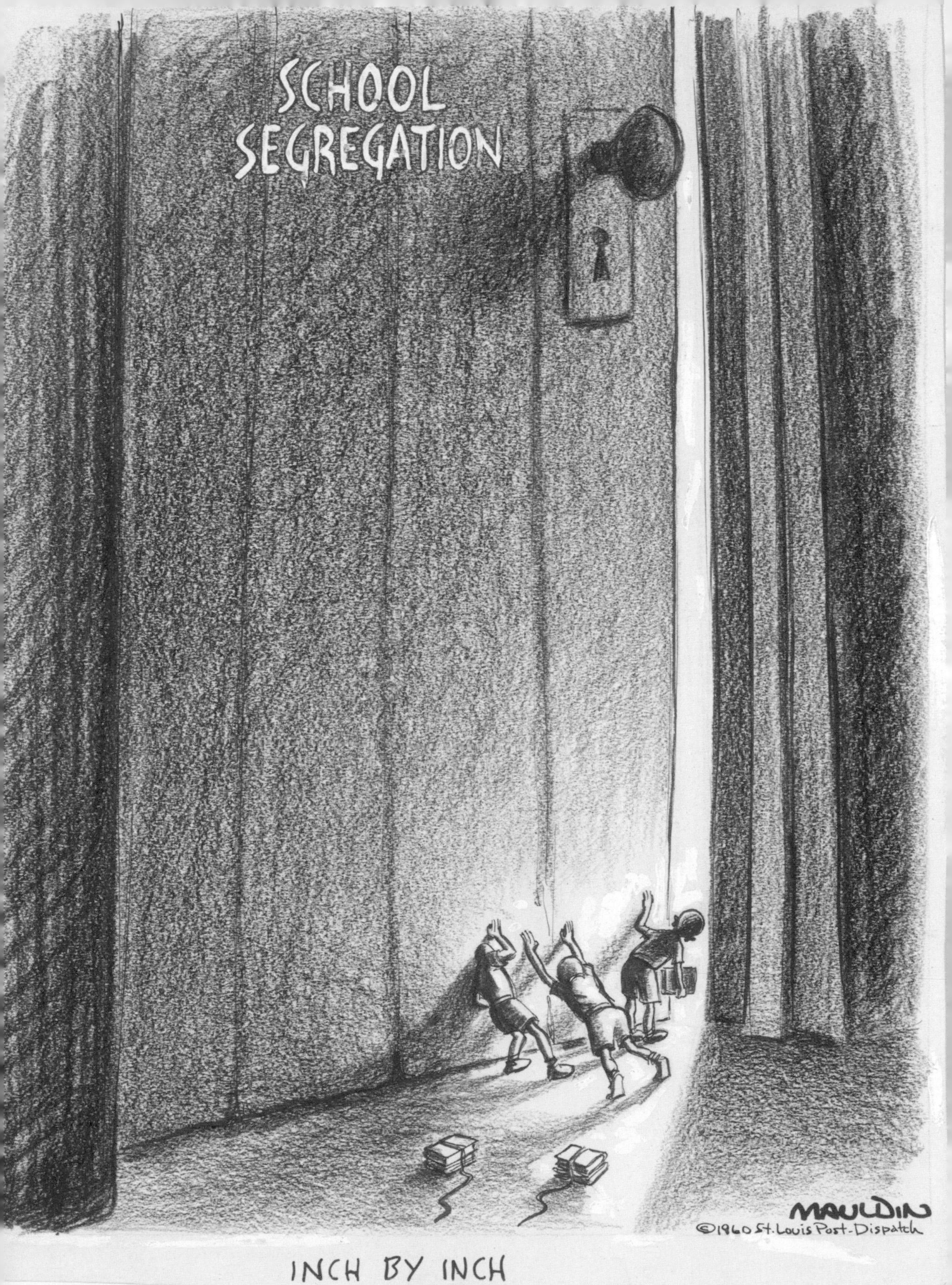
SCHOOL
SEGREGATION
MAULDIN
©1960 St. Louis Post-Dispatch
INCH BY INCH

Sun., April 15, 1962

ST. LOUIS POST-DISPATCH

John F. Kennedy appealed to American industry to keep down inflation. The US Steel Unions agreed to hold down wage demands as long as US Steel kept prices where they were. When US Steel told JFK they were putting prices up $6 a ton, he whipped them into line, earning the tribute above from Bill Mauldin.

"LET'S NOT REPORT IT. THEY'D THINK WE WERE NUTS."

Wed., Feb. 21, 1962

ST. LOUIS POST-DISPATCH

John Glenn becomes the first American to orbit the Earth on 20 February 1962 in *Friendship 7*. This was an important step in restoring prestige to the American space program after Soviet cosmonaut Yuri Gagarin became the first man in space. Soon the US space program would overhaul the Russians in the Space Race.

ABOVE: Like a still from a film, this cartoon by Burris Jenkins shows the possible final moments of film star Marilyn Monroe's life. Monroe was found dead in her bed on 5 August 1962. Although her death was recorded as suicide from a drug overdose, there was a rumor at the time that she had been trying to phone for help.

RIGHT: Like a married couple trying to cram shut a packed suitcase before heading for the airport, John F. Kennedy and Nikita Khrushchev attempt to close the lid on the monster of nuclear war. This is a reference to the Cuban Crisis of 1962, when there was a stand-off over Russian nuclear missiles stationed on Cuba. (Herb Block, 1962)

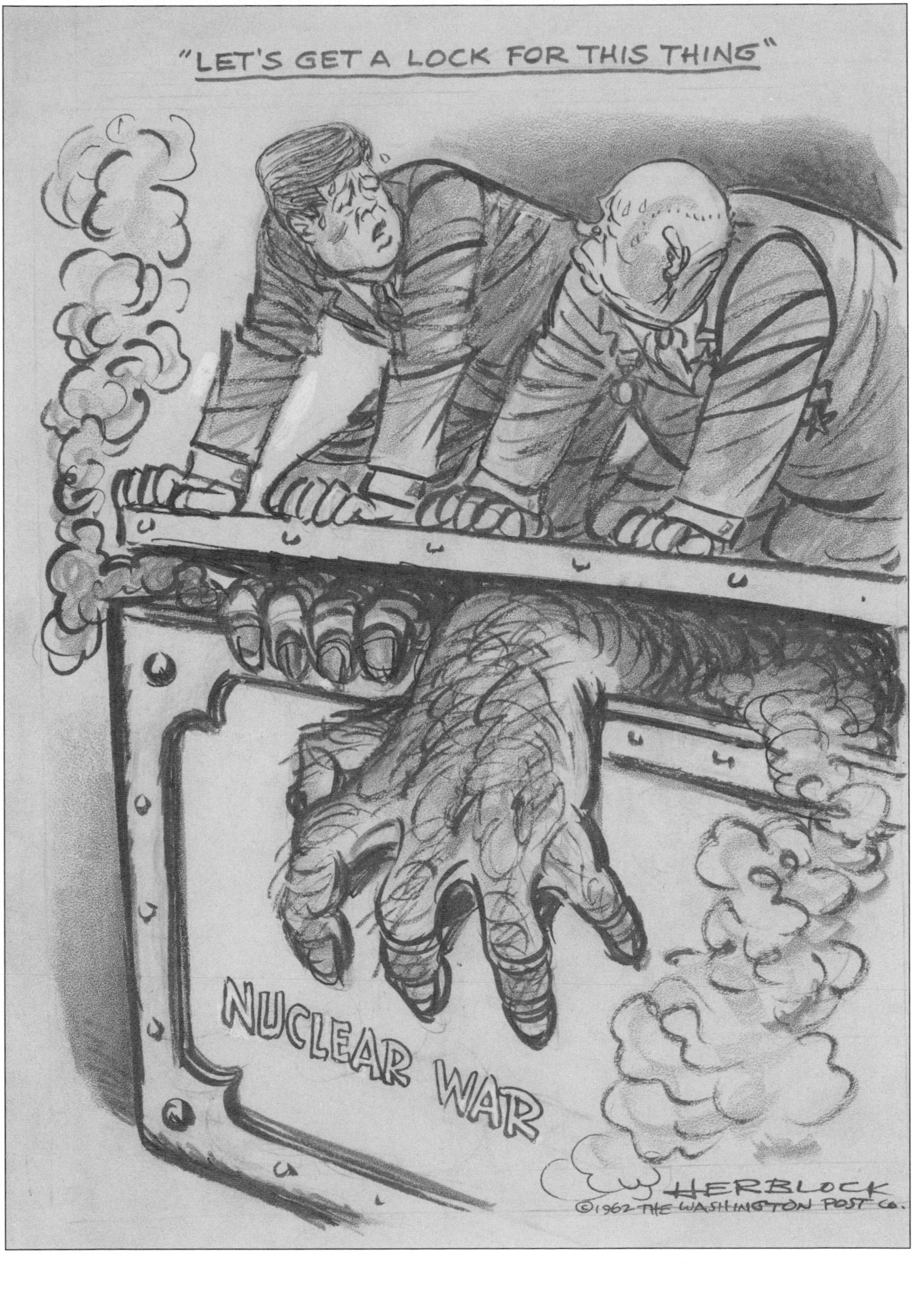
"LET'S GET A LOCK FOR THIS THING"
NUCLEAR WAR
HERBLOCK
©1962 THE WASHINGTON POST CO.

BLASTING HIS WAY OUT? OR FURTHER IN?

The Doctor is Out by Engelhardt (1967)

LEFT: In 1965, US President Lyndon B. Johnson committed a further 50,000 troops to the Vietnam War. 'We will not surrender, nor will we retreat,' he said. At the same time, he called on the UN to increase its efforts to bring about peace. Cartoonist Leslie Illingworth shows LBJ lost in a maze he is trying to reshape with a flame-thrower.

ABOVE: 'The Doctor is Out' by Engelhardt (1967): The words in the title are spoken by a dove to a stork, and the cartoon is a reference to right-wing preacher Norman Peale, who blamed the anti-Vietnam War movement on the children brought up in accordance with Dr Spock's Baby Plan. Peale also wrote *The Power of Positive Thinking*.

ENGRAVED BY STEFAN MARTIN

Ben Shahn

"I DON'T KNOW WHAT WILL HAPPEN NOW. WE HAVE GOT DIF-
FICULT DAYS AHEAD, BUT IT DOESN'T MATTER WITH ME BE-
CAUSE I'VE BEEN TO THE MOUNTAIN TOP. LIKE ANYBODY ELSE
I WOULD LIKE TO LIVE A LONG LIFE. BUT I'M NOT CONCERNED
WITH THAT. I JUST WANT TO DO GOD'S WILL AND HE HAS AL-
LOWED ME TO GO UP THE MOUNTAIN. I SEE THE PROM-
ISED LAND. I MAY NOT GET THERE WITH YOU, BUT I WANT YOU
TO KNOW TONIGHT THAT WE AS A PEOPLE WILL GET TO THE
PROMISED LAND. I AM HAPPY TONIGHT THAT I AM NOT WOR-
RIED ABOUT ANYTHING. I'M NOT FEARING ANY MAN. MINE
EYES HAVE SEEN THE GLORY OF THE COMING OF THE LORD."

Martin Luther King Jr.

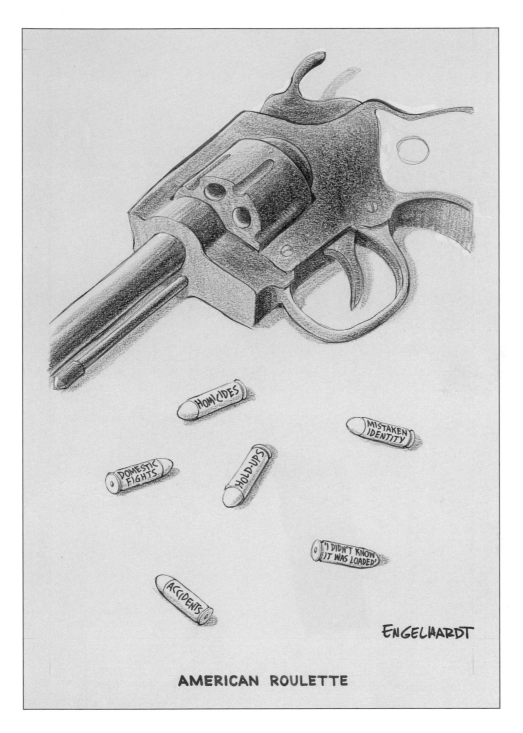

AMERICAN ROULETTE

ENGELHARDT

LEFT: This image of Martin Luther King, Jr. by Ben Shahn was originally commissioned as a cover for *Time* magazine in 1965. Part of the speech, 'I've been to the mountaintop', has been added in memory of King, who was assassinated on 4 April 1968. The speech was delivered in support of striking sanitation workers the day before he died.

ABOVE: The cartoon above by Engelhardt (1971) shows the dangerous game of American Roulette permitted by US gun laws. Ownership of firearms is still one of the most hotly debated issues in the USA. Not much has changed since 1971, except guns have got bigger…

"....AND, OF COURSE, IF CAMBODIA FELL, THEN LAOS WOULD FALL, AND IF LAOS FELL....."

ABOVE: Richard Nixon and a senior US officer walk past a graveyard full of dominoes representing US war dead in this image by Doug Marlette (c.1972). The Domino Theory proposed that if one country in a region became communist, then adjacent countries would soon fall too. This idea was central to US intervention in a number of countries, such as Vietnam, Laos and Cambodia, during the Cold War era.

RIGHT: 'Fall Street' (1992): The growing dependence of the country on financial markets is shown in this Engelhardt cartoon as stocks, bonds and the dollar plummet alarmingly. Each decade seems to have its financial crisis, and no one ever seems to learn…

Above: The Ku Klux Klan in their canteen by Tony Husband (1985). By the 1980s, the era of the organized KKK was all but over, with membership standing at around 5,000. At its peak in 1926, there were 6 million Klan members.

Left: Batting her eyelids at Ronald Reagan who is dressed like a GI, Margaret Thatcher attempts to sell him the British-made Ptarmigan communication system as French President François Mitterrand lurks in the background, doing his best to look just as seductive. Britain and the US have always had a 'special relationship', never better exemplified than during the reigns of Maggie and Ronnie. (by Griffin, 1985)

The Modern World | 189

SEPTEMBER 11, 2001... ANOTHER DAY
THAT WILL LIVE IN INFAMY

TERRORISM

©2001 ENGELHARDT

LEFT: 9/11 was the date when Death had a field day after a co-ordinated spate of attacks on the US by Islamic terrorist group al-Qaeda. Two American passenger planes were flown into the World Trade Center in New York City and the Pentagon was targeted by another hijacked plane. In all, 2,996 people died (including 19 terrorists). America would never be the same again. (2001)

LEFT: Master of the Universe Rupert Murdoch by Ed Murawinski in the *New York Daily News* (2007), a man who is about to demonstrate how many balls he can keep in the air at one time: In 1985 Australian Murdoch became a naturalized American citizen to satisfy legal requirements that only US citizens can own US TV stations. By 2000, Murdoch's News Corporation owned over 50 companies, worth a total of $5bn. In 2015, with a net worth of $13.7bn, he stood at Number 33 in the *Forbes* list of America's wealthiest people.

BELOW: In 2005, Barack Obama, the first African-American to hold the post, became the 44th US President. (by Bill Bramhall, 2009)

Picture Credits

Topfoto: 6, 33 (t), 38-9, 40, 41, 42 (t), 43 (b), 49 (b), 50 (t), 52, 53, 54, 55, 58 (b), 63 (b), 70 (t), 74, 77, 78, 82 (x2), 86, 87, 94, 98, 99, 105 (t), 108, 116, 132, 133, 136, 140, 144, 148, 152, 154, 160, 164 (B), 165, 171

Library of Congress: 7, 10, 11 (x2), 12-3, 15 (x2), 16 (x2), 17, 18 (x2), 19 (x2), 20(x2), 21 (x2), 22(x2), 23, 24 (x2), 25, 26-7, 28 (x2), 30, 31 (x2), 33 (b), 35 (x2), 36, 37 (x2), 42 (b), 43 (t), 47 (x2), 48 (b), 49 (t), 50 (b), 57, 60 (t), 61, 63 (t), 64 (x2), 66 (b), 67 (b), 70 (b), 71 (x2), 73, 75, 76 (x2), 79 (t), 80, 81(x2), 83, 85 (b), 88 (x2), 89, 90, 92-3, 95, 97, 101, 102, 103 (x2), 104 (x2), 105 (b), 106, 107 (x2), 109, 110, 111, 112, 114, 115 (x2), 120-1, 122, 123, 124 (x2), 125, 126, 127, 129 (b), 134, 135, 137 (t), 138, 147, 149, 156-7, 158 (x3), 159, 161, 163, 166, 169 (b), 182, 183, 188 (t), 192

Corbis: 8, 9, 14, 46, 51, 58 (t), 68-9, 91, 130, 170, 186

Getty Images: 29, 44-5, 56, 60 (b), 62, 65, 66 (t), 67 (t), 85 (t), 142, 155, 168, 169 (t), 191 (x2)

Punch: 32, 34, 72, 172, 173, 184, 189 (t)

Mary Evans: 100, 146, 150

Bridgeman: 143

State Historical Society of Missouri: 141, 151, 174, 175, 176 (x2), 178, 179, 180, 181, 185, 187, 188 (b), 190

Flickr: 177

Wikimedia: 48 (t), 96, 113, 117, 129 (t), 131, 145, 153 (t), 162

Art Archive: 59, 79 (b), 139, 167

Mirrorpix: 189 (b)

US National Archives: 84, 128, 137 (b), 164 (t)

'Effects' by John S. Pughe (1903): An old timer draws on his corn cob pipe as he contemplates partaking of a little 'livener' from his bottle of moonshine.